GLIMPSES *of* GRACE

GLIMPSES *of* GRACE

Barbara J. Scott

Xulon Press
555 Winderley Pl, Suite 225
Maitland, FL 32751
407.339.4217
www.xulonpress.com

© 2024 by Barbara J. Scott

All rights reserved solely by the author. The author guarantees all contents are original and do not infringe upon the legal rights of any other person or work. No part of this book may be reproduced in any form without the permission of the author.

Due to the changing nature of the Internet, if there are any web addresses, links, or URLs included in this manuscript, these may have been altered and may no longer be accessible. The views and opinions shared in this book belong solely to the author and do not necessarily reflect those of the publisher. The publisher therefore disclaims responsibility for the views or opinions expressed within the work.

Unless otherwise indicated, Scripture quotations taken from the King James Version (KJV) – *public domain*.

Paperback ISBN-13: 979-8-86850-477-8
Ebook ISBN-13: 979-8-86850-478-5

TABLE OF CONTENTS

Open My Eyes.................................1
The Main Ingredient............................ 2
By Faith 3
What Are You Waiting For? 5
Think on These Things........................... 6
Return to Righteousness! 7
Where Is Thy God?.............................. 9
He Is The Greatest 11
Are You Ready?............................... 12
It Pays to Pray 14
Leave A Legacy of Love 15
Take Some Time Off............................ 16
God Is Our Healer 18
Watch Your Tongue!............................ 20
Pray with Expectation!..........................21
A Heavy Word................................. 22
Do You Resemble Your Father? 23
Keep The Faith 24
Possess Your Possessions........................ 25
The Blood Connection........................... 26
Do You Know Who You Are?..................... 27

God Hears You 28
Do You Know Him? 29
Who's On First? 30
He Will Fix It! 31
Let The Redeemed Of The Lord Say So. 32
Remember Me! 33
Do You Have Benefits? 34
Christ The Solid Rock 35
No Turning Back 36
It's A New Season 37
We've Come Too Far 38
Do Not Forget 39
Full Speed Ahead! 40
Miracles Of God! 41
Don't Look Back 42
Freedom 43
Put Him First 44
He Has Come! 45
What Gift Do You Bring To The King? 46
In His Presence 47
Turn To The Lord 48
Ambassadors For Christ 49
Wait On The Lord! 50
Be Wise Be Ready! 52
The Ultimate Gift 54

Pray With Thanksgiving	55
Be Ye Grateful!	56
He Is Coming Soon	57
No One Greater	58
Taste And See	59
Do You Have A Vision	60
All Things New	63
Oh, Christmas Tree	65
The Light of The World Is Jesus	67
From The Cradle To The Cross	69
Who Is This Jesus?	71
His Name Is, "Wonderful"	73
The Word Made Flesh	75
Jesus Is Our Friend	78
A Thankful Heart	80
What Is Your Theme Song?	82
Sing Unto The Lord	85
Release Strong Faith	87
Do More Than You Can	89
The Miracle Is Within You	91
Rise Up And Walk	93
Come From Under The Circumstances	96
What's In A Name?	98
Activate Your Faith	100
God Will Turn It Around	103

No Camping Here 105
God's Ways Are Not Our Ways. 108
Oh, Worship The Lord. 111
Blessed Assurance 114
Praying Men of God. 116
The Prayers of A Righteous Man 119
God Will Supply. 121
Live In The Truth of God 124
All Things New 126
Mary Didn't Know 128
Jesus Our Savior 130
Do You Know Him?. 132
A Matter of Forgiveness. 134
Against All Odds. 137
Are You Pot Bound? 139
Look Up. 142
Are You Turning Your World Upside Down?. 145
Effectual Prayers. 148
Changed From The Inside Out. 151
A New Creature In Christ 154
Cherish The Moment. 156
Be Strong In The Lord 158
Clutter In The Prayer Closet. 160
Consecrated To God 163
Effective On The Battle Field 165

Detour Ahead	167
Don't Bypass You Pit Stop	169
Don't Bypass Your Pit Stop (2)	172
Empty Vessels	174
Energized by The Presence of God	176
Fit For The Garment	180
God Can And God Will	182
God Has Said, and We Say	185
God's Ways Are Not Our Ways.	188
Grow Where You Are Planted	191
Indescribably Delicious	193
It Is Always Too Soon To Quit	195
Patience Is A Virtue	198
Position Yourself For Transformation	200
It Is Well With My Soul	203
The More We Give The More We Have	206
Preparations For Moving.	209
Keep Your Bag Packed	212
Magnify the Lord	215
Make Every Day A Masterpiece	218
Release Your Potential	221
Resurrection Power	223
Rise Up And Walk	226
The Order of The Towel	228
Having The Mind of Christ	231

Speak to Your Mountain 234
The Majestic Handiwork of God 237
The Light of The World Is Jesus 239
The Right Thirst 241
The Word Made Flesh 245
To Fly Like The Eagle. 248
Touching Jesus With A Purpose. 251
When God Breathes In Your Direction. 255
The Kingdom o God, Here And Now 257
What Kind of Christian Are You? 262
Who Loves Ya', Baby? 265
Rejoice In The Lord 267
Sticks And Stones. 270
Your Miracle Is On Its Way 272
Give It All To Jesus. 275
Life-Changing Prayers. 278
Know God's Power Through Prayer. 281
In Jesus Alone 284
The Father's Handwriting 286
No Weapon 288
Waiting On God 290
The Seasons of Life 293

ACKNOWLEDGEMENT

I acknowledge the blessed Holy Spirit without whose help this book would not have been written. He gave me the words and I wrote them down. I give all glory and honor to Him for His wisdom and guidance.

INTRODUCTION

We see glimpses of the grace of God every day of our lives. It is His grace that awakens us each morning, to give us another day to worship and praise Him. It was not the alarm clock or the voice of someone that woke you up. God gives us just the amount of grace we need for everything He wants us to do. When we truly love the Lord Jesus Christ and follow His Word, His grace abounds more abundantly. Jesus said, "Ask and you shall receive." He said, "Seek and you shall find, knock and it shall be opened unto you." That is His abundant grace. There is nothing we can do to earn it or even be worthy to receive it. It is God's unmerited favor towards us because He loves us.

God opens His hand to bless us at all times. He is always available to us as a Father, a Friend, a Comforter, a Provider, and so much more. Imagine having someone in your life who can be whatever you need Him to be at any time you need Him. That's the grace of God.

The purpose to these messages is to show you the glimpses of God's grace as you experience them in your daily life, walking with Him. Look for them.

God bless you real good!
Barbara J. Scott

> "And God is able to make all grace abound toward you; that ye, always having all sufficiency in all things, may abound to every good work." (2 Cor. 9:8)

OPEN MY EYES

"For ever, O LORD, Thy Word is settled in heaven." (Ps. 119:89 KJV)

Are your eyes open? What do you see? Do you see anything good around you today? Yes, with so much going on in life that is not good, it may be hard to see the good. We must learn to look beyond our physical eyes in order to see that God is still in control, that He is working things out for our good and for His glory. No matter what it looks like, see with the eyes of faith; see what you want to see; see how you want it to be; and see what God says it is, because His Word stands forever! Cling to God's Word and hide it in your heart. It will never change. Don't be afraid to look and see! "Open Thou mine eyes, that I may behold wondrous things out of Thy law." (Ps. 119:18).

THE MAIN INGREDIENT

"But now, O LORD, Thou art our Father; we are the clay, and Thou our Potter; and we all are the work of Thy hand." (Isa. 64:8)

Have you ever baked or cooked something and realized you left out an important ingredient that really needed to be included in what you were making for it to come out right? Imagine a cake without baking powder, a cheese omelet without cheese, cornbread without cornmeal. In life there is one main ingredient we must not leave out if we want things to turn out alright. We wonder why we struggle, why we are up one day and down the next, why our lives just don't pan out the way we want them to. Did you forget the main ingredient, Jesus Christ? There is no life without Him! Have you invited Him to take control of your life? Did you really believe this is your day? "This is the day which the LORD hath made." (Ps. 118:24) Don't leave Him out, He is the One Who makes everything turn out alright. "But seek ye first the kingdom of God, and His righteousness; and all these things shall be added unto you." (Matt. 6:33)

BY FAITH

"All the ends of the world shall remember and turn unto the LORD: and all the kindreds of all the nations shall worship before Thee." (Ps. 22:27)

All through life we put our faith in the things of this world. We have faith that the car will start when we turn the key; faith that that chair will hold you up when you sit on it; faith that the lights will come on when you flick the switch; faith that the airplane will take off and land safely. We never realize how much we do by faith. But when it comes to believing the Word of God, we lack in faith. God's Word is infallible, it will never change, and it will stand forever, yet we choose not to believe it. His Word says that without faith, it is impossible to please Him. When we don't trust His Word we are calling Him a liar, and that God is not true to His Word. When we pray we must believe He hears us and will answer. "And Jesus answering saith unto them, Have faith in God. For verily I say unto you, That whosoever shall say unto this mountain, Be thou removed, and be thou cast into the sea; and shall not doubt in his heart, but shall believe that those things which he saith shall come to pass; he

Glimpses of Grace

shall have whatsoever he saith. Therefore I say unto you, What things soever ye desire, when ye pray, believe that ye receive them, and ye shall have them." (Mark 11:22-24)

WHAT ARE YOU WAITING FOR?

"I will sing of the mercies of the LORD for ever: with my mouth I will make known Thy faithfulness to all generations." (Ps. 89:1)

Do you realize how much time we spend waiting? Think about it. We wait in line in the stores, we wait for traffic lights to change, we wait on corners for transportation, we wait in doctor's offices, and so on and so on and so on, waiting. We even pray and wait on God to answer our prayers, but there is a great benefit in waiting on God. We can be assured there will always be something good coming our way when we wait on God. Don't become impatient, don't run ahead of Him, and don't try to work it out yourself. Wait on Him, His timing is right, He won't be late! Wait with the joy of knowing that God has it in His hand, and He is working it out. He never fails. "But they that wait upon the LORD shall renew their strength; they shall mount up with wings as eagles; they shall run, and not be weary; and they shall walk, and not faint." (Isa. 40:31)

THINK ON THESE THINGS

> "Great is the LORD and greatly to be praised." (Ps. 48:1)

There are so many negative things that come up in our lives and sometimes it may be hard to see past them in order to see the positive and good things happening all around us. God is good and He is always doing good on our behalf, but we have to stay focused on Him so we don't miss the glory. There is an old song of the Church that says, "*Turn your eyes upon Jesus, look full in His wonderful face: and the things of earth will grow strangely dim, in the light of His glory and grace.*" It is so true, if we focus on Jesus and His goodness, we can overcome the negativity and accentuate the positive in our lives. "Finally, brethren, whatsoever things are true, whatsoever things are honest, whatsoever things are just, whatsoever things are pure, whatsoever things are lovely, whatsoever things are of good report; if there be any virtue, and if there be any praise, think on these things." (Phil. 4:8)

RETURN TO RIGHTEOUSNESS!

"I look to the hills! Where will I find help?
It will come from the LORD, who created
heaven and earth." (Ps. 121:1-2 CEV)

You have been raised to life with Christ. Now set your heart on what is in heaven, where Christ rules at God's right side. Think about what is up there, not about what is here on earth. You died to sin, which means that your life is hidden with Christ, Who sits beside God. Christ gives meaning to your life, and when He appears, you will also appear with Him in glory. Don't be controlled by your body. Kill every desire for sexual lusts. Don't be immoral or indecent or have evil thoughts. Don't be greedy, which is the same as worshiping idols. God is angry with people who disobey Him by doing these things. Now you must stop doing such things. You must stop being angry, hateful, and evil. You must no longer say insulting or cruel things about others and stop lying to each other. You have given up your old way of life with its habits, so let the peace that comes from God control your thoughts and be grateful. Let the message about Christ completely fill your life while you use all your wisdom to teach and instruct others.

Glimpses of Grace

"With thankful hearts, sing psalms, hymns, and spiritual songs to God. Whatever you say or do should be done in the Name of the LORD Jesus, as you give thanks to God the Father because of Him." (Col. 3:1-6, 8-9, 15b-17)

WHERE IS THY GOD?

"Behold, I will bring it health and cure, and I will cure them, and will reveal unto them the abundance of peace and truth." (Jer. 33:6)

With all the tragedies and discord going on in this world today, I'm sure many people are asking and wondering, where is God, why doesn't He do something? Where is God? Well, let's think about it for a moment. We took Him out of the schools, we took Him out of the court room, we have taken Him off our jobs, we have taken Him out of public places, we have just plainly told God that we don't want Him around. So, now we need Him to come and help us in all these devastated places. Will He come? He is merciful and gracious, but there is something we must do to show Him that we really want Him in our lives. We must REPENT, ask God to forgive us for pushing Him away because we were satisfied in our sins. He says, "Call unto Me, and I will answer thee, and shew thee great and mighty things, which thou knowest not." (Jer. 33:3). People, it's time, it's past time, to call on the name of the LORD! "If My people, which are called by My Name, shall humble themselves, and pray, and seek

Glimpses of Grace

My face, and turn from their wicked ways; then will I hear from heaven, and will forgive their sin, and will heal their land." (2 Chron. 7:14)

HE IS THE GREATEST

"Our LORD, the nation's will honor You, and all kings on earth will praise Your glory." (Ps. 102:15)

There is no one, no other god, greater than our LORD God Almighty! He alone laid the foundation of the earth and created the heavens. Eventually they will all pass away, but our God will stand forever. He always has been and He will be forever. Who wouldn't want to serve a God like that? He is everything we need, and He is able to give us our heart's desires. He, the Greatest, loves us unconditionally. We can never earn God's love, He does it automatically because He is love, and that's just what He does. When we trust and serve Him there is NOTHING He will not do for us! Love Him, worship Him, honor Him; He is the Greatest! "The LORD forgives our sins, heals us when we are sick, and protects us from death. His kindness and love are a crown on our heads. Each day that we live, He provides for our needs and gives us the strength of a young eagle." (Ps. 103:3-5)

ARE YOU READY?

"Bless the LORD, O my soul. O LORD my God, Thou art very great; Thou art clothed with honor and majesty." (Ps. 104:1)

    We make preparations for everything in our lives but very few of us make preparations for the end of our life here on earth. Do you realize this is not our final home, and that we are just passing through on our journey to our final destination? How we journey through this mortal life will determine where we will spend our eternal life. I know we don't like to think about it, but some of us will leave by way of the grave and some will be alive when Jesus comes back. Did I just say, "When Jesus comes back?" Yes, believe it or not, the Lord Jesus Christ is very soon to come. My question is, will you be ready to go, either way? Everything you see that is going on today is written in the Word of God. The prophecies have been fulfilled concerning the last days, and we are living in the end of the last days. Scary? Not if you have a relationship with God, Who is in control of everything. If you are not ready, I encourage you to get ready now by repenting of all sins and asking Jesus to take over your life. Confess with your mouth that He is Lord and believe in your heart that God has raised Him from the dead. Get ready, get ready, get ready, and live! "Therefore be ye also ready; for in such an hour as ye think not the Son of Man cometh." (Matt. 24:44)

IT PAYS TO PRAY

> "Great is the LORD, and greatly to be praised; and His greatness is unsearchable." (Ps. 145:3)

We all go through so many trials and tribulations in life, which most of them are just a part of being alive in this world. Jesus warned us that these things would happen, but He also said that we are not to worry or fret, but to be happy, because it is all in His hand. If we would just remember to take everything to God in prayer we would have less struggles, and less down time. He tells us we can come boldly to His Throne of Grace in time of need. Why don't we take Him at His Word? The Lord waits for us to come and we make Him our last resort instead of our first thought. There is nothing like being able to have communion with the only One Who can make all things right, and supply all our needs. Take it to the Lord in prayer. "The effectual fervent prayer of a righteous man availeth much." (James 5:16b)

LEAVE A LEGACY OF LOVE.

"I will praise Thee, LORD, with my whole heart; I will shew forth all Thy marvelous works." (Ps. 9:1)

Do you remember your grandparents? Do you remember the things your grandmother taught you about being loving and kind? What about the way she lived her life, showing you what love looks like. Grandparents and parents are the examples to our children that set the course for their lives. What course are you setting, what path will they chose because of the life you lived because of the things they learned from you? We can plant good seeds in our children by teaching them that God is love and how important it is to have a close relationship with Him. Read the Word of God with them, pray with them, take them to Sunday school and church services. These things they will remember for the rest of their lives, as the seeds of love, respect, and faith grow up within them, and they will be able to pass it on from generation to generation. "When I call to remembrance the unfeigned faith that is in thee, which dwelt first in Thy grandmother Lois, and thy mother Eunice; and I am persuaded that in Thee also." (2 Tim. 1:5)

TAKE SOME TIME OFF

"I sleep and wake up refreshed because You, LORD protect me. Ten thousand enemies attack from every side, but I am not afraid." (Ps. 3:5-6)

When is the last time you really took time off from your work-a-day world to relax and enjoy your life? Do you know that if some people couldn't work all the time they wouldn't know what to do with themselves? Some people retire and end up depressed or having a nervous breakdown because their work was their life. God intended for all of us to take time off to rest and relax. He did it after taking six days to make all creation, why don't we think we need to do the same? Take off at least one day a week to give God thanks for the other six days that He gives you life, health, and strength, enabling you to do what you do. Then, take a vacation. Vacate from the ordinary and do something you don't usually do. Visit someone or go someplace you don't usually go, and it doesn't have to cost much at all. Be encouraged, take some time off and use it to give God praise. Jesus has said, "If you are tired from carrying heavy burdens, come to Me and I will give you rest.

Take the yoke I give you. Put it on your shoulders and learn from Me. I am gentle and humble, and you will find rest." (Matt. 11:28-29)

GOD IS OUR HEALER

"The heavens declare the glory of God; And the firmament sheweth His handywork." (Psalm 19:1)

The Word of God, the Holy Bible, tells us that God sent His Word to heal every sickness and disease (Ps. 107:20). He is the great God All Mighty and there is nothing too hard for Him. When you pray, have faith and trust His Word. No matter what negative reports you may receive from doctors, reject them and stand on God's Word. Speak positive words out of your mouth and think positive thoughts. God has not changed; He performed healing miracles in the past and He is still doing it today. Think about it. He is the Creator of our bodies, He made them, so how can we think He cannot fix whatever needs to be fixed. When you purchase something from the store and it breaks down, you are told to send it to the manufacturer. God is the Manufacturer of our bodies, and we go to Him for repair. So, whatever is going wrong in your body or in anyone you know, take it to the Lord in prayer and believe what God has said in His Word. Know that you can trust Him as He watches over His Word to perform it; it will not return back to Him undone. "But He was wounded for our transgressions, He was bruised for our iniquities: the chastisement of our peace was upon Him; and with His stripes we are healed." (Isa. 53:5)

WATCH YOUR TONGUE!

"Great is our Lord, and of great power: His understanding is infinite." (Ps. 147:5)

"Even so the tongue is a little member, and boasteth great things. Behold, how great a matter a little fire kindleth! And the tongue is a fire, a world of iniquity: so is the tongue among our members, that it defileth the whole body, and setteth on fire the course of nature: and it is set on fire of hell. But the tongue can no man tame; it is an unruly evil, full of deadly poison. Therewith bless we God, even the Father; and therewith curse we men, which are made after the similitude of God. Out of the same mouth proceedeth blessing and cursing. My brethern, these things ought not so to be." (James 3:5-6, 8-10). "A doubled minded man is unstable in all his ways." (James 1:8)

PRAY WITH EXPECTATION!

"O taste and see that the LORD is good:
blessed is the man that trusteth in Him."
(Ps. 34:8)

When we lay our petitions before the Lord, first of all we must make sure we are in the right standing with Him. The Word of God says, "If I regard iniquity in my heart, the LORD will not hear me." (Ps. 66:18) We must come with a clean heart, through repentance of all sin. Then we must pray, believing that God will answer our prayers. It is His pleasure to give us the desires of our hearts, but we must have faith to trust that He will do what He says. When you pray, wait on God, don't become impatient. Waiting in prayer is like a pregnant woman who doesn't get tired of carrying the baby, deciding to abort the pregnancy because it is taking too long. She keeps expecting that in due time a baby will come forth. Don't stop praying, don't stop believing, don't stop trusting God! It will happen in due time. The answer is on the way; in God's time. "... Marvelous are Thy works, Lord God Almighty; just and true are Thy ways, Thou King of saints." (Rev. 15:3b)

A HEAVY WORD

"O sing unto the LORD a new song; for He hath done marvelous things: His right hand, and His holy arm, hath gotten Him the victory." (Ps. 98:1)

The Word of God is powerful and can carry a heavy weight. It can lift you up when you are bowed down low. It can carry your burdens when you are weak. The Word of God can give you light when your way seems dark, and it will light up your path when you can't see which way to go. You can find peace and comfort in the Word of God; It is alive and active. There is nothing and no one who can change it; it stands on its own and it stands forever. It is settled in heaven, God spoke it, and He will do everything He has spoken. Are you familiar with the Word of God? Be encouraged and get into God's Word, take hold of it and apply it to your everyday life. Live in it and allow it to live in you! "For the Word of God is alive and powerful. It is sharper than the sharpest two-edged sword, cutting between soul and spirit, between joint and marrow. It exposes our innermost thoughts and desires." (Heb. 4:12). "In the beginning was the Word, and the Word was with God, and the Word was God. And the Word was made flesh and dwelt among us..." (John 1:1, 14a)

DO YOU RESEMBLE YOUR FATHER?

"Let the words of my mouth, and the meditation of my heart, be acceptable in Thy sight, O LORD, my strength, and my redeemer." (Ps. 19:14)

Many children look so much like their father that there is no way they can deny they are his children. They talk like their dad, they walk like him, and they act like him. We have a heavenly Father Who delights to have His children resemble Him in every way, and He will never deny us. He is loving, kind, faithful, forgiving, patient, able to be trusted, and full of joy and peace. Do you see yourself looking like your heavenly Father? Wherever you don't see the attributes and character of your Father manifested in your daily life, pray and ask Him to fill you with Himself. Get into His Word and practice being like Him: practice makes perfect. "Stay close to Me and let My teachings become part of you. Then you can pray for whatever you want, and your prayer will be answered." (John 15:7)

KEEP THE FAITH

> "They shall still bring forth fruit in old age; they shall be fat and flourishing: To shew that the LORD is upright: He is my rock, and there is no unrighteousness in Him." (Ps. 92:14-15)

Our children and young people need our prayers, especially in these last and evil days. They have so many temptations facing them every day! They need our encouragement, they need to know that we as parents, grandparents, great grandparents, and mentors stand behind them pushing them forward to be the very best they can be. We must stand on the Word of God on behalf of our children and youth. Commit them to the Lord and leave them there, and trust that God will make them all that Jesus died to make them be! "And they said, "Believe in the Lord Jesus, and you will be saved, you and your household." (Acts 16:31). "I have been young, and now am old, yet I have not seen the righteous forsaken or his children begging for bread. He is ever lending generously, and his children become a blessing." (Ps. 37:25-26)

POSSESS YOUR POSSESSIONS

"I will praise Thee, O Lord my God, with all my heart: and I will glorify Thy Name for evermore." (Ps. 86:12)

We have many legitimate possessions in Christ Jesus. Here are a few. Salvation: "For God sent not His Son into the world to condemn the world; but that the world through Him might be saved." (John 3:17). Deliverance: "The Spirit of the Lord is upon Me... to preach deliverance to the captives..." (Luke 4:18). Healing: "....And with His stripes we are healed." (Isa. 53:5). Peace: "Peace I leave with you, My peace I give unto you:..." (John 14:27). Joy: "And now come I to thee; and these things I speak in the world, that they might have My joy fulfilled in themselves." (John 17:13). Prosperity: "Beloved, I wish above all things that thou mayest prosper and be in good health, even as thy soul prospereth." (3 John 2). "But upon mount Zion shall be deliverance, and there shall be holiness; and the house of Jacob shall possess their possessions." (Obad. 1:17)

THE BLOOD CONNECTION

> "Bless the LORD, O my soul. O LORD my God, Thou are very great; Thou art clothed with majesty." (Ps. 104:1)

We know what it is to be born into a family and to be adopted into a family. A great number of people find out they have been adopted many years after the adoption, and they feel anger and bitterness toward their adopted parents. Some say they should have been told from the beginning, and some feel less important and loved after they find out. But do you realize that to be adopted is even greater than a biological birth because adoption is a choice. If you were adopted you were chosen to be in that family by your parents; you were born from the heart and not from a sexual encounter. We have been adopted into the family of God through great love. There was a great sacrifice given on our behalf, a Blood sacrifice, and when we acknowledge and receive that sacrifice, we become connected to the family of God by the DNA of our Savior, Jesus Christ. What a phenomenal revelation! "God decided in advance to adopt us into His own family by bringing us to Himself through Jesus Christ. This is what He wanted to do, and it gave Him great pleasure." (Eph. 1:5 NLT)

DO YOU KNOW WHO YOU ARE?

"I will sing of the mercies of the LORD for ever: with my mouth will I make known Thy faithfulness to all generations." (Psalm 89:1).

Because of the Blood of Jesus Christ which He shed for the sins of the world, and because we have received the finished work on Calvary, Almighty God our Father, has lifted us up in high position. He "has made us kings and priests." (Rev. 1:6). He has given us "authority to tread on serpents and scorpions and over all the power of the enemy." (Luke 10:19). We are seated with Christ Jesus in heavenly places. (Eph. 2:6). We are the children of God because we are led by His Spirit. (Rom. 8:14). "Beloved, now are we the sons of God, and it doth not yet appear what we shall be: but we know that, when He shall appear, we shall be like Him; for we shall see Him as He is." (1 John 3:2)

GOD HEARS YOU

> "For ever, O LORD, Thy word is settled in heaven. Thy faithfulness is unto all generations: Thou hast established the earth, and it abideth." (Ps. 119:89-90)

The Word of God says there is not a word that goes out that God does not hear. So, when we are crying out to Him and feel that He isn't listening, just know that God Almighty is not hard of hearing, His ears are not dull. He hears, He knows, and He understands our deepest longings. David said that he cried and the LORD heard him and saved him out of all his troubles. God is the same yesterday, today, and forever, He has not changed, and He is still faithful to His word. God still says that when we call unto Him, He will show us great and mighty things we can't imagine. "And it shall come to pass, that before they call, I will answer; and while they are yet speaking, I will hear." (Isa. 65:24)

DO YOU KNOW HIM?

"I will sing of the mercies of the LORD for ever: with my mouth will I make known Thy faithfulness to all generations." (Ps. 89:1)

Many people profess to know who Jesus is, and really only know "*about*" Him. If you don't have a personal relationship with Him, then you can never really know who He is. Jesus is "King of kings and Lord of lords." (1 Tim. 6:15; Rev. 17:14; Rev. 19:16). There is no one greater than He. He is the "Bread of Life." (John 6:35). All who come to Him will never hunger for the meager things of this world. He is the "Fount of Living Water." (Jer. 2:13; John 4:14). Drink of the water that Jesus gives, and never thirst again. He is the "Good Shepherd." (John 10:11). Jesus watches over His sheep and allows no hurt, harm, or danger to overtake them. He gave His life for His sheep. Do you really know who Jesus is? Who is He in your life? "I Am the Way, the Truth, and the Life: no man cometh unto the Father, but by Me." (John 14:6)

WHO'S ON FIRST?

> "O Come, let us sing unto the LORD: let us make a joyful noise unto the Rock of our salvation. Let us come before His presence with thanksgiving, and make a joyful noise unto Him with psalms." (Ps. 95:1-2)

Many of us enjoy watching a baseball game and get excited when a batter makes it to first base. Sometimes the manager will put in a "pinch hitter" to take the place of a scheduled batter. He knows that the substitute batter may have a better chance of making it "home." There is One Who has made it to first base and has run every base to make it "home" for us. His Name is Jesus and He wants to be on first base in every area of our lives. He wants us to depend on Him to get us to that home plate. Who is batting for you? Who is on first base? "But seek ye first the Kingdom of God, and His righteousness; and all these things shall be added unto you." (Matt. 6:33)

HE WILL FIX IT!

> "It is a good thing to give thanks unto the LORD, and to sing praises unto Thy Name, O most High:" (Ps. 92:1)

In the world, when someone says they need "a fix," we know they are talking about the drugs they are addicted to that are going to give them a "high," lifting them above the cares of this world, that's going to make them "feel better." How many of you know that is not a "fix?" That is only a temporary feel good, and that is really destroying their lives and bringing death to their bodies. "But thanks be to God Who gives us the victory through our Lord Jesus Christ!" (I Corinthians 15:57) There is nothing He cannot do, nothing He cannot fix, if we trust Him and take everything to Him in prayer. When He fixes it, it stays fixed! Hallelujah! Where in your life do you need a "fix" today? What do you need Jesus to do for you? Just pick up the prayer line and call Him up; He will be sure to answer, His line is never busy, He will hear and answer you. "The LORD is nigh unto all them that call upon Him, to all that call upon Him in truth. He will fulfil the desire of them that fear Him: He also will hear their cry, and will save them." (Ps. 145:18-19)

LET THE REDEEMED OF THE LORD SAY SO

> "Our LORD, You are King! Majesty and power are Your royal robes. You put the world in place, and it will never be moved. You have always ruled, and You are eternal." (Ps. 93:1-2 CEV)

As believers in Christ Jesus, He has given us power over all the powers of the enemy. There is no man nor tempting devil we should fear. We should be able to look any devil in the eye in the Name of Jesus, and put it to route. There is power in the Name of Jesus! Use that Name, that Name that gives you the authority to tread on serpents' heads and young lions. Let the enemy know that you know who you are and Whose you are. We are in warfare every day. Step out of bed clad with the "whole armor of God" from head to toe. Stay in your Word, stay prayed up, and spend quiet time with the Father. "Let the redeemed of the LORD say so, whom He hath redeemed out of the hand of the enemy." (Ps. 107:2). "The Name of the LORD is a strong tower: the righteous runneth into it, and is safe." (Prov. 18:10)

REMEMBER ME!

> "It is a good thing to give thanks unto the LORD, and to sing praises unto Thy Name, oh most High: to shew forth Thy lovingkindness in the morning, and Thy faithfulness every night." (Ps. 92:1)

All of us have gone through some trials and tribulations in our lifetime, and that is a part of living on this earth. Jesus told us that we would experience some hard times but be happy in knowing that we are overcomers through Him. Think back over your life about the things the Lord has brought you through, how He has been there to hold you up, strengthen you, and encourage you through His Word. He has not changed. Whatever you may be going through now, our God will see you through. He was with Daniel in the Lion's den; He was in the midst of the fiery furnace with the three Hebrew boys; He spoke, "Peace, be still," to the wind and waves of the tempestuous sea; and He can still do the same for you today. Be encouraged, God has not forgotten you; remember Him. "Jesus Christ the same yesterday, and to day, and for ever." (Heb. 13:8)

DO YOU HAVE BENEFITS?

> "Praise ye the LORD. Praise the LORD, O my soul. While I live will I praise the LORD: I will sing praises unto my God while I have any being." (Ps. 146:1)

Most people know what benefits mean. It could be a profit gained from doing some kind of work, a payment, or a gift. When a person applies for a job one of the main questions he or she asks is, "What is the benefit package?" You want to know about health insurance, vacation time, sick time, short and long-term disability, etc. Did you know we have wonderful benefits when we serve the Lord? We have health insurance because His angels keep us from stumbling and hurting our feet (Ps. 91:11-12; Isa. 43:2). We have the benefit of not lacking any good thing (Phil. 4:19). Make sure you check out your benefits, get in the Word of God, read, and study. We are truly blessed! "Blessed be the LORD, who daily loaded us with benefits, even the God of our salvation. Selah." (Ps. 68:19)

CHRIST, THE SOLID ROCK

> "Everyone on this earth will remember You, LORD. People all over the world will turn and worship You, because You are in control, the Ruler of all nations." (Ps. 22:27)

There is an old hymn of the Church which says, *"On Christ, the Solid Rock I stand, all other ground is sinking sand, all other ground is sinking sand."* As we look at what is going on in this world today, we can see a lot of sinking sand, things we thought were on solid ground are beginning to sink all around us. Our so-called firm foundation is being shaken at the very root. Where can we go, what can we do in this time of trouble? Be encouraged, God is always greater, and He is totally available! We can seek Him anytime, day or night, and know that He is our Protector and everything we need. "From the end of the earth will I cry unto Thee, when my heart is overwhelmed: lead me to the Rock that is higher than I." (Ps. 61:2)

NO TURNING BACK

"Let everything that hath breath praise the LORD!" (Ps. 150:6).

Yes, we have come this far by faith, leaning on the Lord. We have trusted that His Word is true and settled in heaven and no matter what it looks like, how it sounds, or who doesn't believe it, we will not take down, we will not give in, and we will continue to stand firm. We believe God, that it shall be as He has said! We will keep running this race, going on to see what the end will be, expecting to receive the blessings the Lord has promised to those who endure to the end, in this life and in the life to come. "..Let us lay aside every weight, and the sin which doth so easily beset us, and let us run with patience the race that is set before us, looking unto Jesus the author and finisher of our faith;" (Heb. 12:1b-2a)

IT'S A NEW SEASON

"This is the day which the LORD hath made; We will rejoice and be glad in it." (Ps. 118:24)

The Lord woke us up this morning to a brand new day. You didn't live this day yesterday and you won't live this day tomorrow. Today, God is doing a new thing in each of our lives, He is bringing us to a new place in Him. Focus on this very day and discover what new thing is taking place in your life; purposely look for it. "Behold, I will do a new thing; now it shall spring forth; shell ye not know it? I will even make a way in the wilderness, and rivers in the desert." (Isa. 43:19)

WE'VE COME TOO FAR

> "He shall cover thee with His feathers, and under His wings shalt thou trust: His truth shall be thy shield and buckler." (Ps. 91:4)

Most, if not all of us, have come through many trials, tribulations, pain, and sorrow. But we know that we could not have made it without the Lord. Jesus did not say that this would be an easy journey, but He did say that He would be with us every step of the way. Surely, we have come too far to even think about turning around. We must go on to see what the end will be. We have a goal to reach and Jesus is waiting for us at the finish line. We've come this far by faith, and we will continue on to the end! Be encouraged, you can make it! "For we have not an high priest which cannot be touched with the feeling of our infirmities; but was in all points tempted like as we are, yet without sin. Let us therefore come boldly unto the throne of grace, that we may obtain mercy, and find grace to help in time of need." (Heb. 4:15)

DO NOT FORGET

"O sing unto the LORD a new song: sing unto the LORD, all the earth." (Ps. 96:1)

We can all look back over our life and see how far we have come, by the power and grace of Almighty God. He has saved us and brought us over many rough mountains. He has kept us from drowning in the sea of despair, and He has brought us through sickness, pain, and sorrow. He has delivered us out of the hand of the enemy, and He set us up upon high places. Now, you can look back, remember, and be thankful! Don't forget from where you have come, and Who brought you this far along the way. Don't forget to praise the Lord! "I will bless the LORD at all times: His praise shall continually be in my mouth." (Ps. 34:1)

FULL SPEED AHEAD!

> "So we Thy people and sheep of Thy pasture will give Thee thanks forever: We will show forth Thy praise to all generations." (Ps. 79:13)

This is the year of abundance in every way. God is going to be moving quickly and differently, more than ever before in our lives. Be encouraged, put your running shoes on, pull out the throttle and grab hold of God's hand. He is out front moving swifter than a mighty tornado, sweeping our paths, and making a way for us. Don't drag your feet, you don't want to get left behind, you don't want to miss the abundance of blessings that are coming your way. Stay focused like never before and keep your eyes on the prize! "Know ye not that they which run in a race run all, but one receiveth the prize? So run, that ye may obtain." (1 Cor. 9:24)

MIRACLES OF GOD!

> "Who is like unto Thee, O LORD, among the gods? Who is like Thee glorious in holiness, Fearful in praises, doing wonders?" (Exod. 15:11)

In this day and time many people don't believe in miracles, they feel that was for "back then," not now. But the Word of God says that He is the same yesterday, today, and forever; He never changes. Look in the mirror, you will see a miracle of God's grace and mercy. Look back over your life this past year and see how far you have come, see what God has done for you, and give Him the highest praise. Hallelujah! "And be renewed in the spirit of your mind; And that ye put on the new man, which after God is created in righteousness and true holiness." (Eph. 4:23-24)

DON'T LOOK BACK

> "Thou openest Thine hand, and satisfiest the desire of every living thing." (Ps. 145:160)

Have you ever noticed that when runners are running a race they don't look back? They keep their eyes straight, looking for the finish line. Looking back causes you to lose momentum, slowing you down, and could cause you to lose the race. God has great plans for us in our very near future, and we don't want to miss out on anything. Whatever mistakes, pains, heartaches, unforgiveness, or whatever held you down in the past, let it go, put it under the blood of Jesus, stay focused on Him, and keep running full speed ahead. There is a better day ahead! "…And let us run with patience the race that is set before us, Looking unto Jesus the Author and Finisher of our faith…" (Heb. 12:1-2)

FREEDOM

"I will bless the LORD at all times: His praise shall continually be in my mouth." (Ps. 34:1)

Jesus came to set us free from all the things in this life that would hold us down; things that would keep us from living the abundant life that He came to give us. Let us cut loose from all things and people that would hold us back from giving ourselves totally to God and doing His will. The Word of God says to take off every weight and sin that would hold us in bondage. We want to be free to run this race that God has set before us, determined to make it to the finish line. "If the Son therefore shall make you free, ye shall be free indeed." (John 8:36)

PUT HIM FIRST

"Live under the protection of God Most High and stay in the shadow of God All-Powerful." (Ps. 91:1 CEV)

I'm sure all of us can look back over our lives and see things we wish never had happened, mistakes we made, things we should have done, or should have done differently. We have that, "shoulda, coulda, woulda" syndrome. The past cannot be changed, but we can make changes for our future as we continue to move ahead, and the best change we can make that will set everything else in order in our lives is to put Jesus first. Give Him first priority in every area of our lives and let Him take charge. He is so good at taking charge because He knows the end from the beginning, and He knows what is best for us. When we determine to give Him His rightful place in our lives, we can't imagine the blessings God has in store for us. Seek Him through His Word and experience the peace and joy of putting Him first. "With all your heart you must trust the LORD and not your own judgment. Always let Him lead you, and He will clear the road for you to follow." (Prov. 3:5, 6 CEV)

HE HAS COME!

"And behold, Thou shalt conceive in Thy womb, and bring forth a Son, and shalt call His Name JESUS." (Luke 1:31)

Christians and those who are not Christians all over the world, celebrate the birth of Jesus Christ at the end of every year. The songs of His birth are ringing out in the stores, along with other Christmas songs, and every time the praises of Jesus' birth resound through those Carols, hearts are being touched, and the people may not even realize it. Yes, we may not know the exact date of Jesus' birth, but praise God, we do know that He came. He was born into this world, lived, suffered, died, and rose again, so that we might live eternally with Him. Jesus is coming again, very soon. Repent of your sins, believe that He died to save you, and receive Him in your heart, then you too will spend eternity with Him. That is the reason why He came. "For God so loved the world, that He gave His only begotten Son, that whosoever believeth in Him should not perish, but have everlasting life." (John 3:16)

"WHAT GIFT DO YOU BRING TO THE KING?"

> "I will sing of the mercies of the LORD forever: with my mouth will I make known Thy faithfulness to all generations." (Ps. 89:1)

This is the season when we think about giving gifts to those whom we love. As we remember and celebrate the birth of the Savior of the world, do we think about a birthday gift for Him? The greatest gift we could give to the King is ourselves. "All He wants is you, nothing else will do, no just a part, He wants all of your heart, all He wants is you." (Song by Audrey Mieir)) Will you give Him that gift of love today? "I beseech you therefore brethren, by the mercies of God, that ye present your bodies a living sacrifice, holy, acceptable unto God, which is your reasonable service." (Rom. 12:1)

IN HIS PRESENCE

"Thy throne is established of old: Thou art
from everlasting." (Ps. 93:2)

Jesus said that where two or three children of God are gathered together, He is right in the midst of them. The Word of God says that He lives in our praises. It even says He is closer than breathing and nearer than hands and feet. His very presence is with us all the time. His very name is a strong place of refuge where we can run to and be safe. In the Lord's presence we can feel His love that never changes, His peace that the world cannot understand, and His joy that no one can take away. Get to know Him through His Word and live in His presence. "Thou wilt show me the path of life: in Thy presence is fullness of joy; at Thy right hand there are pleasures for evermore." (Ps. 16:11)

TURN TO THE LORD

"Blessed are they that dwell in Thy house:
they will be still praising Thee. Selah."
(Ps. 84:4)

Who do you look to for help? When you are in trouble and the enemy is hunting you down, who do you turn to? When sadness and sorrow are on your trail, who do you go to? When you are afraid and don't know what to do, who do you turn to? The Word of God tells us we can look up to the Lord for help. He is always available and ready to help, anytime day or night. Cry out to Him and He will hear you. "From the end of the earth will I cry unto Thee, when my heart is overwhelmed: lead me to the Rock that is higher than I. For Thou hast been a shelter for me, and a strong tower from the enemy. I will trust in the covert of Thy wings. Selah." (Ps. 61:2-4)

AMBASSADORS FOR CHRIST

"But Thou, O LORD, art a shield for me; my glory and the lifter up on mine head." (Ps. 3:3)

As ambassadors for Christ, we represent the Kingdom of God. Therefore, we should be manifesting the righteousness of God, peace, and joy in the Holy Ghost. Everywhere we go, there should be positive vibes emanating from us. We should be bringing peace in the midst of turmoil, and the joy within us should be flowing out to others, bringing about a change in their lives. All that we say and do should show that we represent the King and His Kingdom. Our very lives should be a mirror of the love, patience, kindness, and goodness of the Lord Jesus Christ. For some, we are the only Bible they will ever read. What are they reading from you as ambassadors for Christ? "Ye have not chosen Me, but I have chosen you, and ordained you, that ye should go and bring forth fruit, and that your fruit should remain: that whatsoever ye shall ask of the Father in My Name, He may give it you." (John 15:16)

WAIT ON THE LORD!

"The LORD is my rock, and my fortress, and my deliverer; my God, my strength, in whom I will trust; my buckler, and the horn of my salvation, and my high tower." (Ps. 18:2)

Being patient and waiting seems to be two of the hardest things to do, especially in this fast-paced world we live in today. Everything is speed up, hurry up, move faster, don't be so slow! Have you ever been driving and had someone speed past you on the wrong side because they felt you were moving too slowly, but only to have to sit and wait at the same red light you are sitting at. People have been rushing to an appointment, or to catch a plane, or just rushing to get somewhere and never making it, because they got into an accident on the way. We need to slow down. We make so many mistakes in life because we rush ahead of God, trying to work it out our way. "What is taking God so long, doesn't He know I'm in a hurry?" God works according to His Own time schedule because He knows the end from the beginning. He knows you are not ready to jump into that marriage, He knows you are not ready for that car yet. He knows He has a better job

Glimpses of Grace

for you, before you consider buying that new home. Yes, God knows all things, that's why He says, "Be still, and know that I Am God..." Sloooowww down, it's all in God's timing, and we can't hurry Him. "Wait on the LORD: be of good courage, and He shall strengthen thine heart: wait, I say, on the LORD." (Ps. 27:1)

BE WISE, BE READY!

> "I will sing a new song unto Thee, O God: upon a psaltery and an instrument of ten strings will I sing praise unto Thee." (Ps. 144:9)

We are living in the last and evil days prophesied in the Word of God. All the signs of this time are written in the Bible, the infallible holy Word of God. Be informed by getting into the Word and reading about the news that is going on in our world today. Be encouraged, you don't you have to be afraid, just put your life in the hand of the One who can fix all things! You can be ready when Jesus returns to take His children with Him. What a glorious day that will be! When you acknowledge that Jesus Christ is Lord and receive Him as your Savior, and believe in your heart that He rose from the dead, you shall be saved. (See Rom. 10:9). That's God's promise to you. If you have not already, be wise and make that confession, and you will indeed be ready. "God.... Hath in these last days spoken unto us by His Son, Whom He hath appointed heir of all things, by Whom also He made the worlds; Who being the brightness of His glory and the express image of His person, and upholding all things by the

Word of His power, when He had by Himself purged our sins, sat down on the right hand of the Majesty on high." (Heb. 1:2-3)

THE ULTIMATE GIFT

"Seek the LORD, and His strength: seek His face evermore." (Ps. 105:4)

We like to give gifts for special occasions like birthdays, anniversaries, graduations, weddings, Valentines Day, and especially Christmas. People everywhere are running hither, thither, and yon, to find the perfect gift for that special someone. We wear ourselves out looking, without even realizing that the greatest gift is only a breath away. Give the gift that keeps on giving, the gift of life. Tell someone about Jesus! That one to whom you want to give a gift may not hear about the love of Jesus unless you tell them. The material gifts we give may get broken, some may fade, some may just get old, but the ultimate gift that God has given us will never change, He is always available to us, always the same. "For God so loved the world, that He gave His only begotten Son, that whosoever believeth in Him should not perish, but have everlasting life." (John 3:16)

PRAY WITH THANKSGIVING

"O give thanks unto the LORD; for He is good: for His mercy endureth for ever. (Ps. 136:1)

Our God is a God of His Word. What he says, He will do. We can trust Him to act on His Word in our lives. When we pray to our heavenly Father, we must thank Him for what we expect Him to do in advance, knowing that He will perform His Word. God's Word will not come back to Him empty, void. It's going to do just what He wants it to do on our behalf. So, by faith we believe that it is already done, and we thank God for the blessing. "Be careful for nothing; but in everything by prayer and supplication with thanksgiving let your requests be made known unto God." (Phil. 4:6)

BE YE GRATEFUL!

"While I live will I praise the LORD: I will sing praises unto my God while I have any being." (Ps. 146:1)

How many of us stopped this morning to say "Thank You" to the Lord for waking us up to a brand new day? Or did you start complaining as soon as you opened your eyes? Have you ever said, "This just is not my day!?" News flash! You were right, no day is our day; it is the Lord's day and He allowed us to be a part of His day. When we awaken in the morning the first thing that we should say is, "Thank You, Lord, for a brand new day, another day to give You glory!" Let's get in the habit of expressing gratitude at the start of each day, and it will go with you throughout your day. You'll find yourself being grateful instead of complaining and being negative or criticizing, finding fault all the time. You will see that things are not as bad as they seem because you gave your day to the Lord and you will have a happy step walking according to His will. "In every thing give thanks: for this is the will of God in Christ Jesus concerning you." (I Thess. 5:18)

HE IS COMING SOON

"Looking for that blessed hope, and the glorious appearing of the great God and our Savior Jesus Christ." (Titus 2:13)

It was prophesied many times in the Scriptures that Jesus Christ our King would come to earth to deliver those who follow Him. He came just as it was told, and over 2000 years ago Jesus said He is coming back again to gather those who are His and take us to heaven to live with Him for all eternity. The Word of God is true, it cannot lie, and it says Jesus is coming again. All the signs of the time indicate that the fulfillment of this prophecy can happen any moment. The stage has been set for the soon coming of our Bridegroom, to take away His Bride, the Church, those of us who have been washed in the Blood of the Lamb by receiving Jesus as our Lord and Savior. Will you be ready? "And, behold, I come quickly; and my reward is with me, to give to every man according as his work shall be." (Rev. 22:12)

NO ONE GREATER

"LORD, Thou hast been our dwelling place in all generations." (Ps. 90:1)

The LORD God Almighty is King of kings and Lord of lords; there is no one greater than He. He is God, all by Himself; He needs no one to speak for Him. Our Lord is the greatest, He is all powerful, He is present everywhere, He knows all things, and there is nothing He cannot do. God is holy and righteous in all His ways, and no one can search Him out. He is creations' Lord, He made us in His own image, and He loves us unconditionally. What a mighty God we serve! And this great God wants to live in our hearts. He wants to have fellowship with us and show how much He loves us. He is our Father and desires our love for Him. He is worthy of all glory, honor, and praise. Let us show our love for the Father today. "Great is the LORD, and greatly to be praised in the city of our God, in the mountain of His holiness." (Ps. 48:1)

TASTE AND SEE

> "Enter into His gates with thanksgiving, and into His courts with praise: be thankful unto Him, and bless His Name." (Ps. 100:4)

Have you ever had your children tell you that they don't like a certain food, and you know they have never tasted it? And you may ask, how do you know you don't like it? We encourage our children to try things they haven't tasted before. Well, have you tasted and seen that the Lord is good? The Word of God encourages us to taste and see. The wonderful thing about that is that when you taste of the Lord, you will see so much more clearly than you have ever seen. It's like having cataracts removed from your eyes. Put Jesus in every situation and circumstance in your life, and you will see how good He is. "O taste and see that the LORD is good: blessed is the man that trusteth in Him." (Ps. 34:8)

DO YOU HAVE A VISION?

You can't have a vision without faith and faith is seeing what is not visible, before you can physically see it. It takes time for a vision to come to fruition; it is a continual process, with God working to do what He needs to do for that vision to take form. Your vision may be to discover a cure for a certain disease, or it could be for education; to establish a school in a foreign country for underprivileged children. Martin Luther King, Jr. had a vision for freedom, that all mankind be treated equally and without violence to obtain that freedom. Your vision may be on a smaller scale, such as being the first one in your family to graduate from high school or college. A vision can be seeing yourself breaking a bad habit. We usually see a vision as something great big, like "washing an elephant." Not all visions are like that. It may be overcoming the fear of modern technology and learning how to use the computer or your smart phone. You may have a vision of how to spend your retirement years, traveling the world, seeing new things and places. To have a vision, one must be committed to hang in there and do whatever it takes to carry out that vision to the end. The vision actually becomes our mission, and we have to set goals and timetables and even guidelines as we take the steps to reach the completion of that vision. Sometimes we set goals that are too far to reach, and we become discouraged and want to quit. Set obtainable, sensible goals that we know we can reach if we work at it and keep trying. The Word of God says that without a vision the people perish. We should all have a vision, something to look forward to that is better than what we have now, better than where we are now; that will make us better than who we are now, and that will be a blessing in other people's lives. Each goal we reach puts us closer to seeing the manifestation of our vision, but we must activate our faith and trust God that it will happen. He gives us help along the way; people and connections we need to progress; resources, and information. He opens closed doors for us to be able to carry out the vision. God doesn't leave us hanging out on our own. He says if we call on Him He will show us great and mighty things that we can't imagine. Jesus had a vision and look what He went through in this life; the trials, tribulations, rejection, and in the end, dying on the cross for the sin of mankind. He did it because He knew He would see the completion of His vision, you and me, with the right to eternal life, because of our faith in Him and His great salvation. That's why He was able to say, "It is finished!" When we have a vision it takes us out of our comfort zone, it requires a lot of hard work, and we have to make sacrifices and be willing to set our priorities in order. Seek the Lord and find out, if you don't know what your vision is, then work at it, stay totally committed, be willing to make whatever sacrifices you have to make, to fulfill that vision. And remember, "By faith we draw it nigh." "Looking unto Jesus the Author and Finisher of our faith; who for the joy that was set before Him endured the cross, despising the shame, and is set down at the right hand of the throne of God." (Heb. 12:2). "Where there is no vision, the people perish." (Prov. 29:18a)

ALL THINGS NEW

> "Remember ye not the former things, neither consider the things of old. Behold, I will do a new thing; now it shall spring forth: shall ye not know it? I will even make a way in the wilderness, and rivers in the desert." (Isa. 43:18-19)

What was your life like last year? Were all of your heart's desires fulfilled? Was it better than the year before? Are there things you wish you could have changed; things you didn't accomplish that you wanted to have done before the new year? Are there things you did that you wish you had not done? As we look back over the past year, we all probably have some things we say we "should of, would of, could of… if only." But the past is now the past and we have been blessed with a new day, a new year, a new future, because God has it in HIS plan for us. He says He will do a NEW thing, and we will know it; He is going to unfold the plan He has for us this year. Don't expect this year to be like last year, that is not God's plan. Look for the great and mighty things that God can do in your life, in the life of your loved ones. Don't miss the blessings, stay alert, stay close to Him, stay in His Word. He has things to say

Glimpses of Grace

to you and to show you. He has new things He wants you to do as you apply His Word to your life each and every day. Yes, you will still have trials and tribulations, that goes without saying, but you are stronger than you were last year. We grow in grace from year to year as we learn more, as we understand more of the ways of the kingdom of God. As you read and study the Word of God, you will see what you didn't see last year, and you will understand what you didn't understand the year before. That's because you have grown to be more like Jesus!

All things new!!! That's what the Father is doing; so be ready to move when He says move; be ready to go where He says go; be ready to speak when He says speak; be ready to do what He says do. We must be totally involved in His new thing, in total obedience to His will. "And He that sat upon the throne said, Behold, I make all things new, And He said unto me, Write: for these words are true and faithful. And He said unto me, It is done. I Am Alpha and Omega, the beginning and the end. I will give unto him that is athirst of the fountain of the water of life freely, He that overcometh shall inherit all things; and I will be his God, and he shall be my son." (Rev. 21:5-7)

OH, CHRISTMAS TREE

I know, Christmas is past, so why am I writing about a Christmas tree? Well, let's not forget about Christmas so quickly. If you were like me, you sang a lot of Christmas carols. I understood the meaning of the Christmas carols like I have never done before; even after singing them and knowing them by heart for many years. Many people, especially some Christians feel that the Christmas decorations are worldly and insignificant. But if you listen to the Holy Spirit and let Him teach you about the decorations, you will learn that they are very significant to the birth of Jesus and why He came to earth (of course, I am not talking about anything that has to do with Santa Claus). If you know the true meaning of Christmas you know that Jesus came into the world to die for us, that we might be saved from sin, from the wrath of God because God hates sin. Jesus indicated to His disciples how He would die, but they didn't grasp hold of Him being crucified on a cross. Jesus told them, "As you know, Passover begins in two days, and the Son of Man will be handed over to be crucified." (Matt. 26:2). It went right over their heads. Jesus had to die on a cross, that is why the Romans had to be the ones who carried out the death sentence that the Jews laid upon Jesus. Crucifixion was the Roman way of execution for their criminals. You see, it was all a part of the prophecy being fulfilled. The Jewish law stated that anyone who was hung on a tree was cursed in the sight of God. (See Deut. 21:23). Jesus became a **CURSE** for us by going to the cross. Notice too, that the tree we decorate at Christmas time is an Evergreen tree; it lives year-round, year in and year out. This tree represents **EVERLASTING LIFE**. Our Savior Jesus Christ shed His precious Blood on a tree, thereby becoming a curse for us, so that we should not perish but have eternal life. What a miracle of God's grace and mercy. *"O Christmas tree, O Christmas tree, how lovely are thy branches…"* "But Christ has rescued us from the curse pronounced by the law. When He was hung on the cross, He took upon Himself the curse for our wrongdoing. For it is written in the Scriptures, "Cursed is everyone who is hung on a tree." (Gal. 3:13 NIV)

THE LIGHT OF THE WORLD IS JESUS

Jesus came into a world full of darkness, dark with rampant sin and no regard for Almighty God. He came to be a Light in our darkness. "In Him was life; and the life was the light of men. And the Light shineth in darkness; and the darkness comprehended it not." (John 1:4-5). Think of a room with gross darkness, no light shining anywhere. Then, someone comes in and lights a match, a tiny match, and that darkness has to give way to the light of that match. If this could happen with a very small match, how much more can the Light of Jesus push back the darkness in our lives. The darkness in that room had to acknowledge the light had come, and so we must acknowledge that Jesus, the Light of the world, has come. He wants to shine in our lives with His love, joy, and peace. In Him is no darkness at all, He is the true Light, which lighteth every man (See John 1:9). Jesus says whoever follows Him will never again walk in darkness. He gives new life; life to the blind, the lame, the deaf, and the sinner who He died for. When we obey Him and His way, He, the Sun of Righteousness, shines in our lives and ultimately lives His life through us.

If only the world would turn to Jesus and receive the finished work on Calvary, what a change it would be in each of our lives. The Word of God says that Jesus is our Light and our Salvation and that we don't have to fear anyone or anything; He is the strength of our life. There is no one greater than our Lord and Savior Jesus Christ. Isn't it wonderful to know that all we have to do is trust Him and know that His Word is true? He is everything we need in life. Let Jesus light up your life. Will you let Him in to be the everlasting light (See Isa. 60:19), the Light that was sent to lighten the Gentiles? (See Luke 2:32). "For You are the fountain of life, the light by which we see." (See Ps. 36:9)

FROM THE CRADLE TO THE CROSS

Christmas isn't over until God says it's over. Who would have thought that a baby in a manger cradle would make such an impact on the world. And yet, baby Jesus did just that. God Almighty stepped down from His glory and wrapped Himself in the flesh of mankind to deliver us from the slavery of sin. What great love! No one loves us that way. He could have come as a great king, but He chose to come as a humble little baby boy, the same way all babies are born into the world, through the womb of a woman. And then Jesus lived His life on earth going through all the temptations and the trials, that a male child goes through throughout his life. Jesus knew what it was like to be a toddler, a young child, a teen, and a young adult. He is our example in life, and we can't say He doesn't understand what we go through. We will never suffer as He did for us. He was hated, rejected, and bullied, even by His own brothers and sisters, and He did not deserve any of it. Many times we cause our own pain and suffering, but Jesus didn't do that. This was Emmanuel, "God with us," on His way to the cross, the cross of redemption for all mankind. There was no turning back for Jesus, He came to die, and nothing could have made Him change His mind. This was the Father's plan to bring us back to Him. Jesus knowing all things, knew how much He would have to suffer in order to bring us back to the Father, but He was willing to do the Father's will. He said, "Nevertheless, not what I will, but what Thou wilt." (Mark 14:37). It was indeed a long journey for Jesus, but He pulled His strength from the Father as He continuously stayed in contact with Him through prayer. Whatever Jesus did, He was doing only what the Father told Him to do. As we go through this journey of life, we too must keep in constant contact with the Father, pulling our strength from Him. He is the strength of our lives, and we don't have to be afraid of anything.

There is nothing the Father will not do to get us through every tunnel, over every mountain, and through every valley in life to make it to the other side. He wants us to reach the finish line and with Him on our side, we will win, we will make it "home." We must keep our eyes lifted up unto the hills where our help comes from; knowing that we can do all things through Christ Who strengthens us. Jesus made it to the from the cradle to the cross, and now the ball is in our court. Don't drop it, stay in the game, and keep running to the end. "To him that overcometh will I grant to sit with Me in My throne, even as I also overcame, and Am set down with My Father in His throne." (Rev. 3:21)

WHO IS THIS JESUS?

When Jesus walked the earth, the people wanted to know just who He was. Some knew Him to be Joseph's Son, the carpenter. Others knew Him to be Mary's Son out of wedlock, so they thought. Some knew Him to be a good teacher. Others who saw His miracles knew Him to be a Miracle Worker. But who is He really? God has many Names, and Jesus is just one of them. Whatever God's Name is, that is who He is and what He does. His Names are His attributes. He can be in your life whoever you need Him to be. A refuge in time of trouble, a strong tower when you need a fortress, a healer when you are sick in your body, or a light when your way is dark, and you cannot see. Who is He in your life? Jesus is a way-maker, He can make a way out of no way. He is certainly a miracle worker, and He does what no other one can do. Jesus always keeps His promises; He never fails what He says He will do, He always does just that, and we can trust Him. Jesus is our Savior and the Lover and Bishop of our souls. He loves us unconditionally. His Name means, Savior, and He saves us in all kinds of situations and circumstances. We can call upon His Name and know that He will hear and answer us, day, or night. He is awesome in all His ways and His ways are past finding out. We can't figure

Glimpses of Grace

Him out; we can't know what He is thinking and what He will do. He says His ways are higher than our ways and His thoughts are higher than our thoughts. There is no way our finite minds can match His infinite mind. He is Jehovah God, King of kings, and Lord of lords. He is the Great I Am that I Am.

"One day Jesus asked His disciples, "Who do people say the Son of Man is?" They replied, "Some say John the Baptist; others say Elijah; and still others, Jeremiah or one of the prophets." "But what about you?" He asked. "Who do you say I am?" Simon Peter answered, "You are the Messiah, the Son of the living God." Jesus replied, "Blessed are you, Simon son of Jonah, for this was not revealed to you by flesh and blood, but by My Father in heaven.""" (Matt. 16:13-17 NIV). Who do you say that Jesus is?

HIS NAME IS, "WONDERFUL"

"His Name is Wonderful, His Name is, Wonderful, His Name is, Wonderful, Jesus, my Lord.

He is the Mighty King, Master of everything, His Name is, Wonderful, Jesus, my Lord.

He's the Great Shepherd, the Rock of All Ages, Almighty God is He. Bow down before Him, Love and adore, His Name is Wonderful, Jesus, my Lord." (Song by Audrey Mieir)

Jesus is marvelous, He is whatever His Name says. He is "marvelous in all His works, and that my soul knows right well." (See Ps. 139:14). We loosely use these words to describe people we are impressed with and really, no one is all that. We can only be speaking the truth when we say those things about Jesus because that is who He is. He is "awesome in all His ways and His ways are past finding out." (See Romans 11:33-36). He is incredible, there are really no words to fitly describe His greatness, His wonderfulness, His might, and His power. And it is when we celebrate special days, that we remember just Who Jesus is. After the celebration is over, we go back to our everyday lives, many not even giving Him a second thought. How can we do that to our Great God and King?!

Glimpses of Grace

We sit in worship services and the pastor has to encourage the people to give God praise, raise our hands and worship Him, thank Him for our blessings. The God Who gives us life and breath each and every day, and someone has to tell us to thank Him? To give Him praise? Imagine how He must feel about us who say we love Him! This is Jesus, our wonderful Savior and He loves us above all that He has created.

We say we love Him, but do we really? Jesus had a reason for asking Peter three times do you love Me. Do we love Him above all persons, places, and things in this world? Have we really given our all to our Savior, or just on special days? Jesus gave His all for us, His very life; that's what makes Him so wonderful. And now, let us play it forward and make a new commitment to Jesus our wonderful Savior, giving Him our all, every day. "Wherefore God also hath highly exalted Him, and given Him a Name which is above every Name: That at the Name of Jesus every knee should bow, of things in heaven, and things in earth and things under the earth; And that every tongue should confess that Jesus Christ is Lord, to the glory of God the Father." (Phil. 2:9-11)

THE WORD MADE FLESH

"In the beginning was the Word, and the Word was with God and the Word was God. The same was in the beginning with God. All things were made by Him; and without Him was not anything made that was made. And the Word was made flesh, and dwelt among us, (and we beheld His glory, the glory as of the only begotten of the Father,) full of grace and truth." (John 1:1-3, 14)

The Word says that when God created the world, Jesus was right there with Him. When He said, "Let us make man in Our image," Jesus was right there with Him. (See Gen. 1:26). God has always existed in three Persons, God the Father, God the Son (Jesus), and God the Holy Spirit. As you read and study the Word of God (the Bible) you will see all three Persons of the Trinity working at different times. The Gospel of John says that nothing was made without Jesus. When God created, He spoke everything into existence. He said, "Let there be" and it was. As He spoke, that was Jesus creating things into existence. "So God created man in His Own image, in the image of God created He him; male and female created He them." (Gen. 1:27). (The Word is speaking to someone right here.)

When Jesus entered into the world He entered as the Word of God. That is why He kept saying, "The words I speak, I'm not speaking on My Own, I speak whatever the Father tells Me to speak." (John 7:16, John 12:49). Jesus is still speaking in these last days, and we must heed what He is saying. In days past God spoke to man through His prophets, but now He is speaking through His Son, Jesus. We have Jesus' example as He walked this earth and we have the written Word, the Bible. "Hath in these last days spoken unto us by His Son, Whom He hath appointed heir of all things, by Whom also He made the worlds; Who being the brightness of His glory, and the express image of His Person, and upholding all things by the Word of His power, when He had by Himself purged our sins, sat down on the right hand of the Majesty on high;" (Heb. 1:2-3)

Jesus, our Creator, came in the flesh, lived, suffered, bled, and died; then rose again. He is now seated at the right hand of the Father, praying for us. (See Rom. 8:34). There is power in His Words when He speaks them, and power in His Words when we speak them. There is power in our own words when we speak them, so be careful what you let out of your mouth. Speaking Jesus' Words will always bring encouragement and hope. Jesus lives within us, and He speaks through us; so open your mouth and let Him fill it with Himself. You will be surprised what a difference we will make in the lives of others when we do. "For the Word of God is quick, and powerful, and sharper than any two-edged sword, piercing even to the dividing asunder of soul and spirit, and of the joints and marrow, and is a discerner of the thoughts and intents of the heart." (Heb. 4:12). (Jesus the Word, knows everything.)

JESUS IS OUR FRIEND

When you look at Facebook you see that some people have hundreds of friends, or so it seems. Just how do you define a friend and how can one person have so many? The dictionary defines "friend" as someone with whom you have a bond with who is not a relative or sexual partner. Webster says, "one attached to another by affection or esteem." That's a good one. Or how about the Urban Dictionary, "A friend is someone you love and who loves you, someone you respect and who respects you, someone whom you trust and who trusts you. A friend is honest and makes you want to be honest, too. A friend is loyal. …A friend is someone who tells you if you're being stupid, but who doesn't make you feel stupid. …A friend is someone for whom you're willing to change your opinions. A friend is someone you look forward to seeing and who looks forward to seeing you.." Hundreds of "friends," I don't think so. In order to be a true friend you have to really get to know that person. You have to develop a loving, caring relationship with that person; be willing to go out of your comfort zone to help in time of need; someone who can cheer you up when you are sad; and someone you can tell your dearest secrets to and know they will not tell anyone else. A friend is someone who

Glimpses of Grace

will laugh with you when you laugh and cry with you when you cry. A friend is someone who will lend you things, money, even their clothes and then tell you that you don't have to pay it back. How many friends did you say you have?

Jesus calls us His friends, and He is more than we could ever imagine a friend to be. He was willing to lay down His life for His friends (us). "Greater love hath no man than this, that a man lay down his life for his friends." (John 15:13). He said we are His friends if we do what He commands us to do. And what does He want us to do? "This is My commandment, That ye love one another, as I have loved you." (John 15:12). Proverbs says that there is a friend that sticks closer than a brother. (See Proverbs 18:24). There are brothers and sisters who are not as close and loving as some of those we call our friends. Jesus shared His life with His friends. He told them and is still telling us things He heard from His Father. "But I have called you friends; for all things that I have heard of My Father I have made known unto you." (John 15:15b). Jesus chose us to be His friends. Are you being a true friend to Jesus? How well do you know Him? (See John 15:16-17)

A THANKFUL HEART

The Word of God tells us over and over again that we are to be thankful in every circumstance in our lives whether we feel it is a blessing or not, because no matter what happens, God is in it working on our behalf. He knows what is best for us and is always working it out for our good and for His glory. He wants us to give Him all our cares because He cares for us; there is nothing in our lives that He is not concerned about. So be thankful, giving Him praise and glory, standing on your faith that it is working for your good!!!

Recently, I came across this prayer to God of someone thanking Him for all His blessings even though they have not manifested yet. This is certainly a prayer that we can attach to our lives as we show God that we are thankful.

"Dear God:

I want to thank You for what You have already done. I am not going to wait until I see results or receive rewards; I am thanking You right now. I am not going to wait until I feel better or things look better, I am thanking you right now; I am not going to wait until people say they are sorry or until they stop talking about me, I am thanking Your right now. I am not going to wait until the pain in my body disappears; I am thanking You right now. I am not going to wait until my financial situation improves; I am going to thank You right now. I am not going to wait until the children are asleep and the house is quiet, I am going to thank You right now. I am not going to wait until I get promoted at work or until I get the job, I am going to thank You right now. I am not going to wait until I understand every experience in my life that has caused me pain or grief; I am going to thank You right now. I am not going to wait until the journey gets easier or the challenges are removed. I am thanking Your right now. I am thanking Your because I am alive. I am thanking You because I made it through the day's difficulties. I am thanking you because I have walked around the obstacles. I am thanking You because I have the ability and the opportunity to do more and do better. I am thanking You because You have not given up on me." Author unknown

What prayers do you have on the altar, and what are you waiting for the Lord to do in your life or your loved ones'? Start thanking Him right now for the answers that are on the way.

"In everything give thanks; for this is the will of God in Christ Jesus concerning you." (I Thess. 5:18). "O give thanks unto the LORD; for He is good: for His mercy endureth forever." (Ps. 136:1)

WHAT IS YOUR THEME SONG?

"Make a joyful noise unto God, all ye lands: Sing forth the honour of His Name: make His praise glorious. Say unto God, How terrible art Thou in Thy works! Through the greatness of Thy power shall Thine enemies submit themselves unto Thee. All the earth shall worship Thee, and shall sing unto Thee; they shall sing to Thy Name. Selah." (Ps. 66:1-4)

Have you ever awakened in the morning with a song singing in your spirit? The Lord has given you a song in the night season and you wake up with that song singing in your very soul. God has given you *victory* while you were asleep, He has *delivered* you from something and given you a song in the "night season." Because He never slumbers nor sleeps, He is constantly working in us while we don't even know it. David was constantly singing songs to the Lord. When he was being pursued by King Saul, or by his son, Absolom, he would cry out unto the Lord asking God to deliver him from His enemies. He said, "Lord, they are trying to eat up my soul, do something, Lord, get them off my trail. They gather themselves together against me; they laugh at me, they want to see me fall. How long, Lord, are Your going to let this go on?" And then David would say, "I will sing unto the Lord; I will sing praises unto our God." (See Ps. 13:1-6). God wants to put a song in your heart. He has a song for every season. When you have been disappointed and let down by someone you thought you could trust, God will give you this song: *"My hope is built on nothing less than Jesus' Blood and righteousness; I dare not trust the sweetest frame, but wholly lean on Jesus' Name. On Christ the solid Rock, I stand – all other ground is sinking sand, all other ground is sinking sand."*

Sometimes you may be in a knock-down, drag out battle with the enemy where you are fighting for the soul of your husband, or your children have gone astray, and it seems like you are losing the battle. Then you read in the Word of God, "(For the weapons of our warfare are not carnal, but mighty through God to the pulling down of strong holds;) Casting down imaginations, and every high thing that exalteth itself against the knowledge of God, and bringing into captivity every thought to the obedience of Christ." (2 Corinthian 10:4-5). Then, you hear the song singing in your soul, *"A mighty Fortress is our God, A bulwark never failing; Our helper He amid the flood of mortal ills prevailing. …And tho this world, with devils filled, should threaten to undo us, We will not fear, for God hath willed His truth to triumph thru us. The prince of darkness grim, We tremble not for him – His rage we can endure, For lo, his doom is sure: One little word shall fell him.*" And that Word is, JESUS! At the Name of Jesus, devils fear and fly. That is our weapon against the enemy. The Gospel of Jesus Christ is entwined in the songs we sing. That's why when we hear anointed singing it stirs our very soul. So, sing your songs unto the Lord, He wants to hear them. We sound like angel voices to Him. Paul told the church in Colosse to, "Let the word of Christ dwell in you richly in all wisdom; teaching and admonishing one another in psalms and hymns and spiritual songs, singing with grace in your hearts to the Lord." (Col. 3:16)

SING UNTO THE LORD

> "Make a joyful noise unto the LORD, all
> ye lands. Serve the LORD with gladness:
> Come before his presence with singing."
> (Ps. 100:1-2)

Do you know that the angels in heaven are always singing and rejoicing, praising God? They are always joyful, so they sing praises to the Lord, and they worship Him with their songs. What is your favorite song? A song that you always find yourself singing and don't even realize that you are singing. That's your theme song because it brings you comfort and peace. I believe David's theme song may have been Psalm 34 because he said he would bless the LORD all the time, no matter what was going on in his life. "I will bless the LORD at all times: His praise shall continually be in my mouth." (Ps. 34:1). David trusted God in season and out of season, no matter whether he was in trouble or in quiet times.

This may be your season for going through some hard times right now. You may have done all that you can do trying to get a loved one saved or delivered. You've worn yourself out and then you hear this song singing deep down in your soul, *"What a Friend we have in Jesus,*

All our sings and griefs to bear! What a privilege to carry Everything to God in prayer! O what peace we often forfeit, O what needless pain we bear, All because we do not carry everything to God in prayer!" (Joseph M. Scriven). And you say, Lord, I give it all to You; You fix it as only You can do! And then you hear this song, *"Be still, my soul! The Lord is on thy side; Bear patiently the cross of grief and pain; Leave to thy God to order and provide, In every change He faithful will remain. Be still, my soul! Thy best, thy heavenly Friend thro' thorny ways leads to a joyful end."* (Jean Sibelius)

    What is your theme song today? Do you want to know what my theme song is? *"Blessed assurance, Jesus is mine! O what a foretaste of glory divine! Heir of salvation, purchase of God, Born of His Spirit, washed in His Blood. This is my story, this is my song, Praising my Savior all the day long; This is my story, this is my song, Praising my Savior all the day long."* (Fanny Crosby). No matter what is going on in your life, whether it is sorrow, sadness, joy, or gladness, let the Lord give you a song to sing; and sing a song of praise to Him. "O come, let us sing unto the LORD: let us make a joyful noise to the rock of our salvation." (Ps. 95:1). "O sing unto the LORD a new song: sing unto the LORD, all the earth. Sing unto the LORD, bless His Name; show forth His salvation from day to day." (Ps. 96:1-2)

RELEASE STRONG FAITH

We wonder why the apostolic miracles are not present in our congregations today as in the days of old. We don't see the lame coming in and laying down their crutches and walkers and getting out of wheelchairs. Why is that? What is the difference in our churches today? Jesus said, "According to your faith be it unto you." (See Matthew 9:29). According to *your faith*, according to how much faith you release into the atmosphere, "be it unto you." We have to trust God with every nerve, and every atom of our being. We say we do but God knows that we don't: we stand on the shore casting out a fishing rod, when God wants us to cast off from the shore, launch out into the deep, let down our nets, and bring in the miracle blessings we are praying for. The problem certainly is not God doing His part; He is still performing miracles today. The problem is the Church's weak faith. Faith doesn't need to "see" to believe; faith sees because it believes. (See Matt. 9:28-30)

Jesus prayed for the Father to glorify Him that He may glorify the Father. (See John 17:1). And when that glory fills the temple, the sanctuary; fills our bodies which are the temple of the Holy Ghost; our faith is released into that glorious atmosphere, then the miraculous power of God is manifested, and bodies are healed, souls are delivered,

Glimpses of Grace

and captives are set free. Faith is like a mustard see – small but strong, and grows into a big tree, able to be a home and shelter for many birds. Jesus did not perform all of His miracles the same way. We argue and give up when we don't see what we expect to see and how we expect to see it. Trust God's Word. We have to go deeper in our faith; know that Jesus is who He says He is. He made the sea, He made the fish and put them in the sea, and He knows just where He put them. So launch out into the deep, let down your net, and expect to see the manifestation of the glory of the Lord. "Now when He had left speaking, He said unto Simon, Launch out into the deep, and let down your nets for a draught. ..Nevertheless at Thy word I will let down the net." (Luke 5:4 & 5b)

DO MORE THAN YOU CAN

Jesus said, "I am the vine, ye are the branches: He that abideth in Me, and I in him, the same bringeth forth much fruit: for without Me ye can do nothing." (John 15:5). In order to bring in "much" fruit there is a stipulation Jesus put forth. First, we must abide in Him. Abide, what does that mean? We must live in Him and stay where we live. We can't be roaming around out of our dwelling place and expect Jesus to go looking for us. He is only going to look in one place, and that is in Him. We must be in close relationship with Him doing His will. He must be living His life through us, otherwise we are no good to Him. "If a man abide not in Me, he is cast forth as a branch, and is withered; and men gather them, and cast them into the fire, and they are burned." (John 15:6)

When we are not abiding in Jesus we are going off on our own way, and there are many ditches on that path. "Trust in the LORD with all thine heart; and lean not on your own understanding. In all thy ways acknowledge Him, and He shall direct thy paths." (Prov. 3:5-6). Jesus said there is nothing we can do without Him. It doesn't matter how smart we think we are, how much education we have, or how much we have prospered without Jesus; it amounts to a big fat "0" in His sight. But whatever we do in His Name, He blesses it abundantly and prospers us in every way. He uses us for His glory and souls are saved, bodies healed, minds delivered from the bondage of addictions, and so much more.

Doing good works out of the will of God will not bring His good favor upon us. Jesus says, "Many will say to Me in that day, Lord, Lord, have we not prophesied in Thy Name? and in Thy Name have cast out devils? And in Thy Name done many wonderful works? And then will I profess unto them, I never knew you: depart from Me, ye that work iniquity." (Matt. 7:22-23). We cannot do God's work without abiding in Jesus; it is unacceptable. Jesus says we must obey His Word and keep His commandments. We can do more if we live in Him and allow Him to live in us. We can do so much more than we ever dreamed we could do. Jesus said that we would do greater works than He did. With the empowerment of the Holy Ghost, it is possible, but we cannot bypass Jesus and expect to do the greater works. The Holy Ghost is the One Who enables us to live in Jesus, and He is Jesus living in us. He takes the things of Jesus and shows them to us. We cannot bombard our way to the Father and ignore Jesus. He is the only way to the Father, and He will be our Judge in the end. But with Jesus, we can do all things. "I can do all things through Christ Who strengthens me." (Phil. 4:13)

THE MIRACLE IS WITHIN YOU

We are all miracles of God's grace and mercy. God takes what He has made of us to be used for His glory. Then we can be a miracle in someone else's life. "The Spirit of the Lord God is upon me; because the LORD hath anointed me to preach good tidings unto the meek; He hath sent me to bind up the brokenhearted, to proclaim liberty to the captives, and the opening of the prison to them that are bound; to proclaim the acceptable year of the LORD, and the day of vengeance of our God; to comfort all that mourn; To appoint unto them that mourn in Zion, to give unto them beauty for ashes, the oil of joy for mourning, the garment of praise for the spirit of heaviness; that they might be called trees of righteousness, the planting of the LORD, that He might be glorified." (Isa. 61:1-4). There is someone waiting for their miracle. Are you available to God today? What has He done for you? Think about it. In your time of sadness and sorrow, did you see the miracle of God's strength in your life? God is a very present help in time of trouble. (See Ps. 46:1). Have you seen God's miracle in your time of sickness; how He healed your body, took away the pain? "But He was wounded for our transgressions, He was bruised for our

Glimpses of Grace

iniquities: the chastisement of our peace was upon Him; and with His stripes we are healed." (Isa. 53:5). When you needed provisions for your family, God provided exactly what you needed. Did you see that miracle? "But my God shall supply all your need according to His riches in glory by Christ Jesus." (Phil. 4:19). He used people in your life to work His miracles.

God uses us to be miracles in the lives of others, to work His will in their lives. We are His hands and His feet in this world. "I can do all things through Christ which strengtheneth me." (Phil. 4:13). He works His will through us as we align our wills to His will. Are you willing to do God's will in the earth, so others may see the manifestation of the miracles they are praying for? "For it is God which worketh in you both to will and to do of His good pleasure." (Phil. 2:13). Jesus said that the works He did was the Father in Him working through Him. He also said, "greater works than these shall we do if we believe." (John 14:10-12). Christ in us the hope of glory, it is He in us working through us with His miracle working power. "Even the mystery which hath been hid from ages and from generations, but now is made manifest in His saints: To whom God would make known what is the riches of the glory of this mystery among the Gentiles; which is Christ in you, the hope of glory: whom we preach, warning every man, and teaching every man in all wisdom; that we may present every man perfect in Christ Jesus." (Col. 1:26-28)

RISE UP AND WALK

When Peter and John were going into the temple to pray, there was a lame man who had been lame all his life. He reached out to Peter and John for them to give him money. Peter's response to the man was, "Look on us." The man did as he was instructed, expecting to receive money from Peter and John, but he received more than he expected. Peter told him that he had no money to give him, but what he had he would give him that. Peter was filled with the power of the Holy Ghost, and the works that Jesus did he was able to do also. This is what Jesus meant when He said that we would do greater works than He did on the earth. When Peter said, "In the Name of Jesus Christ of Nazareth rise up and walk," that man did not hesitate to take Peter's hand and get up from the ground. (See Acts 3:1-16). And Peter with holy boldness did not doubt that Jesus would heal the lame man. What faith and confidence on the part of both Peter and the lame man! How many of us would have had that kind of faith and trust in God?

In order for the power of God to be made manifested in the lives of those we touch, we must first believe in our hearts that God will do what He says He will do. Jesus said if we believe and not doubt in our

Glimpses of Grace

heart, that we could ask what we want, and it will be given unto us. We have to rise up and walk the walk of faith before we can help someone else. And the confidence is not in ourselves, but in the living God. Jesus said that whatever we ask in His Name, the Father will give it unto us. As believers in Christ Jesus, filled with the Holy Spirit, we have that same power within us that Peter and John had. Would you be willing to say to someone, "Rise up and walk," knowing that they had been born lame? We think about what *we can do* and doubt that it will happen for us. Jesus is Jehovah Rapha, He is the Healer, but He is willing to use us if we make ourselves totally available to Him. We must rise up and walk in the faith of the Son of God who loved us and gave Himself for us. In Him we live and move and have our being. Absolutely, we can do nothing without Him. But thanks be to God who gives us the victory to be able to do all things through Christ who strengthens us.

God will not give His glory to another, and when the people ran to Peter and John because they saw the lame man walking, Peter said to them, "Why are you looking at us as though we by our own power or holiness made this man walk?" (Acts 3:12). He let them know that it was the man's faith in Jesus that healed him. Activate your faith, rise up and walk in the Name of Jesus, so that that lame person in your life may be able to grab hold to your hand and by faith, and get up off the ground and walk, too. "If you abide in Me, and

Glimpses of Grace

My words abide in you, you shall ask what you will, and it shall be done unto you. Herein is My Father glorified, that you bear much fruit; so shall you be My disciples." (John 15:7-8)

COME FROM UNDER THE CIRCUMSTANCES

Have you ever asked someone how they are doing, and their reply was, "I'm doing fine under the circumstances"? When someone replies that to me, I say, "What are you doing under the circumstances, you should be on top of them?" Of course, they look at me like I'm crazy, but think about it. With God as our Father, our Provider, our Strong Tower, our Refuge and Strength, why should we be UNDER our circumstances? He is our very present help in time of trouble; He is our joy and peace in the midst of the storms of our life if we give it all to Him to handle. "Cast all your anxiety on Him because He cares for you." (I Peter 5:7). "Do not be anxious about anything, but in every situation, by prayer and petition, with thanksgiving, present your requests to God. And the peace of God, with transcends all understanding will guard your hearts and your minds in Christ Jesus." (Phil. 4:6-7). We can be on the top of every situation with God by our side. "If God be for us, who can be against us?" (Rom. 8:31). God is always greater!

Imagine if you were facing a fiery furnace as the three Jewish young men, Shadrach, Meshach, and Abednego. If anyone could be UNDER their circumstance, it certainly would have been them, but they weren't, they were bold with faith! They told King Nebuchadnezzar that they knew God was able to deliver them. (See Deut. 3:16-18). As a result of their faith, those young men saw God right in the midst of the fire with them. He keeps His promises, He never fails. "He will call on Me, and I will answer him; I will be with him in trouble." (Ps. 91:15)

What is your problem today? What circumstances have come up that you feel you just cannot deal with? Whatever you do, don't get under them! Use your spiritual weapons and overcome them with the **Word of God**. Search the Scriptures and see what God has said about that situation, and say what He says. Put it under the **Blood of Jesus** and declare the victory. Call on the **Name of Jesus** to dispel your anxieties and seek the peace of Jesus that passes all understanding. People in your life will wonder how you can be so calm with all that is going on. Then, you can tell them you are no longer UNDER your circumstances; you have given them all to Jesus and He has them under His control.

We serve an awesome God and there is nothing too hard for Him. Let Him handle every situation, invite Him in, and watch Him take over. "The LORD will make you the head, not the tail. If you pay attention to the commands of the LORD your God that I give you this day and carefully follow them, you will always be at the top, never at the bottom." (Deut. 28:13)

WHAT'S IN A NAME?

Do you know what your name means, what it stands for? Parents name their children all kinds of names for different reasons. Maybe it just sounds nice, or someone in the family has that name, or it was the name of a grandparent or close relative. Whatever the reason, that child has to live with that name for the rest of their life, whether they like it or not, unless they decide to legally change it.

The name Jabez means *"pain"*; his mother named him that because she had pain when he was born. (I Chron. 4:9). It's a wonder he wasn't in pain all of his life, but God blessed him! Jacob was named so because he was trying to come out of his mother's womb first by grabbing hold of his brother, Esau's heel. (See Gen. 25:24-26). Jacob's name means *"supplanter,"* one who takes over on purpose, in the place of another. And that is the kind of life Jacob lived; he was a conniver, a trickster; but God changed his name to, "Israel." (See Gen. 32:24-30; 35:10). Names are important and significant. Parents must choose wisely what they name their children, because children can live up to their names, good or bad.

There is One who has truly lived up to His Name; His Name is, Jesus. Joseph was told by the angel that he was to name Him *"Jesus"* because He will save His people from their sins. (See Matt. 1:21). God had a plan and a purpose for Jesus' Name in the earth. Jesus lived, suffered, bled, and died to save us from our sins; and then rose again. Now He is seated at the right hand of God the Father, interceding for us: and there is no other name under the heaven given to men that can save us: only the Name, *"JESUS."* "Jesus, the Name high over all, in hell and earth or sky. Angels and men before it fall, and devils fear and fly." Song by Charles Wesley). There is power in the Name of Jesus! "Therefore God exalted Him to the highest place and gave Him the Name that is above every name, that at the Name of Jesus every knee should bow, in heaven and on earth and under the earth, and every tongue acknowledge that Jesus Christ is Lord, to the glory of God the Father." (Phil. 2:9-11)

If you don't know, search to see what your name means, or find out where it originated from. Some names were just made up by our parents, and in some cases, because our fore parents couldn't spell, they misspelled the name and gave it a different meaning. Whatever your name is now, it will change when we stand before Jesus in heaven. He has a new name for all of us. He says, "Whoever has ears, let them hear what the Spirit says to the churches. To the one who is victorious, I will give some of the hidden manna. I will also give that person a white stone with a new name written on it, known only to the one who receives it." (Rev. 2:17 NIV)

ACTIVATE YOUR FAITH

"Now faith is the substance of things hoped for, the evidence of things not seen." (Heb. 11:1). God expects us to live by faith. He has given all of us a measure of faith so that we can walk by faith and not by sight. "But without faith it is impossible to please Him: for he that cometh to God must believe that He is, and that He is a rewarder of them that diligently seek Him". (Heb. 11:6). Being a Christian, a follower of our Lord Jesus Christ, is a faith walk. Over and over again during Jesus' ministry He told those to whom He ministered, "According to your faith be it unto you" (Matt. 9:29), "Your faith has made you whole" (Matt. 9:22), "Great is thy faith." (Matt. 15:21-28), "And Jesus seeing their faith saith unto to sick of the palsy, Son, your sins are forgiven" (Mark 2:5). Jesus encourages us to have a persistent faith, keep asking, don't give up, don't doubt.

Faith without works is dead, we must activate our faith, and do something to show that we believe God, so He will do whatsoever we ask. You need a job and are praying for God to open a door for you. Then go out and put in applications, expecting God to answer your prayer. Your wayward children are not listening to you as you try to lead them in the right way. Put them in the hands of

Jesus by faith and prayer and leave them there; expecting them to be saved. "Yea, a man may say, Thou hast faith, and I have works; shew me thy faith without thy works, and I will shew thee my faith by my works. But wilt thou know, O vain man, that faith without works is dead?" (James 2:18; 20)

Our faith is made perfect when we move on what we believe God to do. We don't just sit on our hands doing nothing. When Elisha told to widow woman to get as many jars as she could borrow from her neighbors, she didn't ask him if he was crazy. She acted on faith, believing that God was going to bless her through the prophet. When she began to pour from the little pot of oil she had into the vessels, all the jars were filled with oil. She had enough to sell and pay her debt and more than enough to live on. (See 2 Kings 4:1-7). Sometimes God gives us instructions of what to do to activate our faith. Don't question Him, just do what He says. Naaman went to Elisha to be healed of leprosy and was told to wash in the Jordan River seven times. He was indignant at first, then he obeyed and was healed immediately. His indignation turned to faith. (See 2 Kings 5:10-14).

We can't go by what our natural eyes see, we have to see with our spiritual eyes; see the invisible as though it is visible. We don't need faith for what we can see, we need faith for what we can't see. When we don't put our faith in action, it means we don't trust God; and if we don't trust Him who has all things in His hand, then we are closing ourselves off from the blessings He wants to give us. "For whatsoever is born of God overcometh the world: and this is the victory that overcometh the world, even our faith." (1 John 5:4)

GOD WILL TURN IT AROUND

Joseph was Jacob's son by his wife Rachel. Joseph was Jacob's favorite son, and he didn't mind letting his other sons know it. Joseph also had dreams which were really prophecies from God, concerning his brothers and father bowing down before him. This made his brothers hate him and they end up selling Joseph to some Ishmaelites who were on their way to Egypt. Things really looked bad for Joseph, but God had a plan for him. (See Gen. 37 and 39). In spite of Joseph being falsely accused and thrown into prison for a long time, God turned it around, gave him great favor, and raised him up to a high position in Egypt, where he was able to help many to survive a famine, including his father, his brothers, and all their family. "And Pharaoh said unto his servant, Can we find such a one as this is, a man in whom the Spirit of God is? And Pharaoh said unto Joseph, Forasmuch as God hath shewed thee all this, there is none so discreet and wise as thou art: Thou shall be over my house, and according unto thy word shall all my people be ruled: only in the throne will I be greater than thou. And Pharaoh said unto Joseph, See, I have set thee over all the land of Egypt." (Gen. 41:38-41)

Glimpses of Grace

It doesn't matter how dark your path may seem to be, hold on to your faith. Joseph never blamed God for the hard times he experienced, he continued to trust Him to bring him out. The Bible doesn't even say anything about him hating his brothers for what they did to him. Instead, he let God use him right where he was. And because of his obedience and love for God, never turning his back on God, God turned things around for Joseph and blessed him abundantly. He is the same God who will work in your situation and turn things around for you. Trust Him with all your heart and believe His Word. "Behold, I am the LORD, the God of all flesh. Is there anything too hard for Me?" (Jer. 32:27)

God is no respecter of persons, and He doesn't love Joseph any more than He loves us. He will do the same for any one of His children. "What shall we then say to these things' If God be for us, who can be against us?" (Romans 8:31). Expect God to turn it around for you, for your good and for His glory!

NO CAMPING HERE

"The LORD is my light and my salvation; whom shall I fear? the LORD is the strength of my life; of whom shall I be afraid?" (Ps. 27:1). Have you ever been fearful of a human being? Some people have enemies who will try to hurt them physically. Elijah was one who had enemies and one was a woman, the king's wife, Jezebel. After Elijah had won a great victory in getting rid of the prophets of the idol god, Baal, Jezebel vowed to kill him. (See I Kings 18 and 19). Elijah was literally afraid and eventually ended up hiding in a cave, and God asked him what he was doing in that cave.

Watch out for the enemy after you have received a great victory or deliverance from the Lord. Satan knows he is defeated and now he will try to sow discouragement in your mind. This can happen especially if you are tired and worn out from battling the enemy, which was probably the case with Elijah. He even prayed for God to take his life; Elijah needed a refreshing from the Lord, and God sent angels to feed him and give him water to drink. After that, he was able to travel for 40 days and nights to Horeb, the mount of God. It was there he found the cave and stayed there, but God did not allow him to stay in that cave, he still had work to do.

Glimpses of Grace

There are times when we may feel like giving up and going into retirement from doing the work of the Lord, especially when we have enemies pursuing us, physically and spiritually. But God is the One who tells us when our time is over and He encourages us to keep trusting Him, that He has our back. Listen to what David said about his enemies, "When I cry unto Thee, then shall mine enemies turn back: this I know; for God is for me. In God have I put my trust: I will not be afraid what man can do unto me." (Ps. 56:9; 11). Now is not the time for finding a cave and camping out from the enemy. Remember, we are more than conquerors because we are always fighting from the winning side. Don't listen to the enemy telling you that you need to quit. It is always too soon to quit. Wear him out, put on the whole armor of God, and get back into the battle. There is no such thing as AWOL (Absent Without Leave) in this war! "(For the weapons of our warfare are not carnal, but mighty through God to the pulling down of strong holds:) Casting down imaginations, and every high thing that exalteth itself against the knowledge of God, and bringing into captivity every thought to the obedience of Christ;" (2 Corinthians 10:4-5).

Whatever you need to win, God has already provided for you. You will not lack anything, every soldier in God's army is well equipped to fight and win. Just know that whatever and whoever your enemy may be, we don't have to camp out in a cave for fear because God said He will cover us with His feathers and His Word shall be our shield

Glimpses of Grace

and buckler. Trust His Word, it will stand forever, it is settled in heaven, and it will not change. "No weapon that is formed against thee shall prosper; and every tongue that shall rise against thee in judgment thou shalt condemn. This is the heritage of the servants of the LORD, and their righteousness is of Me, saith the LORD." (Isa. 54:17)

GOD'S WAYS ARE NOT OUR WAYS

God is an awesome God, and the Bible says that His ways are impossible for us to figure out. Our minds are too finite to be able to figure out the God who made the Universe, but sometimes we try to do it anyway. When we pray and expect Him to answer, we have it all planned who we want Him to answer, and we have the nerve to get upset if it doesn't come out the way we planned. But God is omniscient, He knows everything, and He knows what is best for us. He answers our prayers in the way He knows is best for us. You may have been praying for a certain job and didn't get it, and later you found that the company shut down. God already knew, and He always has something better in mind.

Have you ever followed your GPS and it suddenly wanted to take you in another direction, and you begin to complain and fuss wondering why it changed direction? So, you don't follow the GPS, you continue going in the same direction. Then, you get down the highway and find that there is a backup in traffic because of an accident and wish you had gone the way the GPS was telling you to go. We do that with God, don't we? We say, *"God can't be telling me to go this way, or do it this way, or say it this way, because that is not what I had planned."* The Word of God says that we make plans, but God is the One who carries them out. We must learn to trust Him in everything, not just some things that seem easy, but in the hard things where there are disappointments, and we can see no way it will work out for us. The Lord our God tells us that His ways are not our ways, He doesn't think the way we think. "For My thoughts are not your thoughts, neither are your ways My ways, saith the LORD. For as the heavens are higher than the earth, so are My ways higher than your ways, and My thoughts than your thoughts." (Isa. 55:8-9)

God knew us before we were born into this world. He has special plans for each of us and He knows what He has to do to carry out those plans, and He is going to do it His way. We make choices in life, some good and some bad, some right and some wrong. God always gives us chances to get it right and to follow His will for us. How do we know His will? I'm glad you asked. God's will is His Word. Read it, study it, meditate on it, and apply it to your life, and you won't go wrong. There is an old hymn of the church which sums it up so plainly:

> *"God moves in a mysterious way His wonders to perform; He plants His footsteps in the sea*
>
> *And rides upon the storm.*

Deep in unsearchable mines Of never failing skill He treasures up His bright designs And works His sovereign will.

Ye fearful saints, fresh courage take; The clouds you so much dread Are big with mercy and shall break In blessings on your head.

Judge not the Lord by feeble sense, But trust Him for His grace; Behind a frowning providence, He hides a smiling face." William Cowper, 1773.

"*His purposes will ripen fast, Unfolding every hour; The bud may have a bitter taste, But sweet will be the flower.*

Blind unbelief is sure to err And scan His work in vain; God is His own interpreter, And He will make it plain." William Cowper, 1774.

"And we know that all things work together for good to them that love God, to them who are the called according to His purpose." (Rom. 8:28)

OH, WORSHIP THE LORD

"O worship the LORD in the beauty of holiness; fear before Him, all the earth." (Ps. 96:9). When God gave the Commandments to Moses, the first one He gave was, "Thou shalt have no other gods before Me." (Exod. 20:3). He made us to worship and praise Him, to give Him glory and honor. God wants to establish an intimate relationship with human creation. He made us in His image for that purpose. He made us with all of His goodness in us and a love for Him, but all that changed in the Garden of Eden when Adam and Eve sinned against God. Now we must seek Him to get back into that right relationship with Him. By an act of our will, we must choose to turn to God, repent of our sins, and accept the price that was paid on Calvary for our redemption: then we can fully worship and praise Him. We will be able to tell of His greatness and love for all mankind. "Give praise to the Lord, proclaim His Name; make known among the nations what He has done." (Ps. 105:1 NIV)

Jesus taught that we must love the Lord our God with all our heart, soul, and mind. (See Matt. 22:37). When we love Him with our total being, we will have no problem worshiping Him. God is a jealous God and He will not stand for us to worship anyone or anything other than He. "How great you are, Sovereign Lord! There is no one like You, and there is no God but You, as we have heard with our own ears." (2 Sam. 7:22 NIV). People worship many gods in this world, but there is only ONE TRUE GOD, the LORD God Jehovah, Maker of heaven and earth. And you know what? It doesn't matter who believes it or not, that doesn't make it any less true. God always has been and always will be. He is from everlasting to everlasting, and worthy of all worship and praise. "For from Him and through Him and for Him are all things. To Him be the glory forever! Amen." (Rom. 11:36 NIV). "But the hour is coming, and is now here, when the true worshipers will worship the Father in spirit and truth, for the Father is seeking such people to worship Him. God is Spirit, and those who worship Him must worship in spirit and truth." (John 4:23-24 ESV). We must worship Him with all of our innermost being, nothing half-hearted; because God knows what is in our heart, He made us, and His Spirit is in us; we can't fool Him.

Glimpses of Grace

God loves us unconditionally. He cares for us and takes care of us; there is nothing He would not do for His children; and He is alive for evermore. Why would we worship something or someone who can do nothing for us, not even express their love for us; cannot speak, see, or hear, and are not even alive? Why would we not want to worship God and God alone? "Oh come, let us worship and bow down; let us kneel before the LORD, our Maker!" (Ps. 95:6)

BLESSED ASSURANCE

Assurance means a guarantee, a promise; something we can declare with confidence. The old hymn of the church says, *"Blessed assurance, Jesus is mine; oh, what a foretaste of glory divine."* Wow! Just think about all the wonderful things the Bible says that Jesus is. He is our Savior, our Fortress, our Strength, our Good Shepherd, our Provider, our Healer, our Peace, He is our Elder Brother, we are joint heirs with Him, He is our Bread, He is our Living Water, and we could go on and on. This is the confidence we have in who Jesus is in our lives. And this is just a little bit of what heaven is like, as we experience heaven here on earth.

Have you experienced the Lord Jesus Christ in the truth of who He is? He is all this and much more, and we can have the blessed assurance that who He is, is what He does, and He is ours. Jesus said we can ask the Father for anything in His Name and the Father will give it to us. "If ye abide in Me, and My words abide in you, ye shall ask what ye will, and it shall be done unto you." (John 15:7). Jesus said, "All things that the Father hath are Mine: therefore said I, that He shall take of Mine and shall shew it unto you." (John 15:15). We belong to Jesus and He belongs to us. What a marvelous revelation! God is our Father, and we can go to Him for anything; we can ask for anything that lines up with His will for our lives. Remember, God's will is His Word, so we don't have to be in the dark about what His will is for us, just get into the Word and see what He has said. His Name is *"Faithful and True."* That means we have the guarantee that He keeps His promises, and He will not fail us. Can we say that about ourselves in our relationship with Him?

We serve an Awesome God!! There is no one like Him. "There is none holy as the LORD; for there is none beside Thee: neither is there any rock like our God." (I Samuel 2:2). Oh, how He loves you and me; He cares, oh yes, He cares!!! "For I know the thoughts I think toward you, says the Lord, thoughts of peace and not of evil to give you a future and a hope." (Jer. 29:11). "Are not two sparrows sold for a copper coin? And not one of them falls to the ground apart from your Father's will. But the very hairs of your head are all numbered. Do not fear therefore; you are of more value than many sparrows." (Matt. 10:29-31). God has a plan for each one of us. "But you are a chosen generation, a royal priesthood, a holy nation, His own special people, that you may proclaim the praises of Him who called you out of darkness into His marvelous light." (1 Peter 2:9). No one loves us like He does. *"Blessed assurance, Jesus is mine. O what a foretaste of glory divine. Heir of salvation, purchase of God, Born of His Spirit, washed in His Blood."* Fanny Crosby, 1873.

PRAYING MEN OF GOD

Do you ever wonder why you see so many more women in the church than you see men? Even married women are there without their husbands. Jesus came to earth as a male child and the devil hates men more than anything. He does everything he can to destroy the male seed born into this world. Look at our prisons, the crack houses, the bars; there you see mostly men and our male youths. Yes, there are women and young girls caught up in these vices of Satan, but God has a special calling on the male. In the Garden of Eden, Adam was the first who God created, and He gave Adam dominion over all the earth, over every living thing. What happened to man and the authority God gave him? Sin! (See Gen. 1:26-3;1-24.)

God, being a just and holy God, made a way for men to get back to Him through Jesus Christ our Lord and Savior. "For God so loved the world, that He gave His only begotten Son, that whosoever believeth in Him should not perish, but have everlasting life." (John 3:16). That's it, men! The second Adam, Jesus Christ, has come to redeem you, the first Adam. Now you have access to take your rightful place in this earth and be the men that Jesus died to make you. God is calling for you first of all in your homes, in the church, on your jobs, in our government; our children need you in their schools. "According to the eternal purpose which He purposed in Christ Jesus our Lord: In who we have boldness and access with confidence by the faith of Him. That He would grant you, according to the riches of His glory, to be strengthened with might by His Spirit in the inner man; That Christ may dwell in your hearts by faith; that ye, being rooted and grounded in love, May be able to comprehend with all saints what is the breadth, and length, and depth, and height; And to know the love of Christ, which passeth knowledge, that ye might be filled with all the fulness of God." (Eph. 3:11-2; 16-19)

We are living in very evil times, I'm sure you can all see and understand. God wants to use you men to be His instruments in this world; to be His hands and feet, to be His voice speaking His Word, to stand up and be counted for the cause of Jesus Christ, and to get down on their knees and pray down the power of God. Are you willing? Make that commitment to Jesus, first of all, receiving Him as your Lord and Savior if you haven't done so already. "Now therefore fear the LORD and serve Him in sincerity and in faithfulness." Put away your sins, "and serve the LORD. ...choose this day whom you will serve." Let your war cry be, "But as for me and my house, we will serve the LORD." (See Josh. 24:14-15). This is God's promise to you, "Have not I commanded thee? Be strong and of a good courage; be not afraid, neither be thou

Glimpses of Grace

dismayed: for the LORD thy God is with thee whithersoever thou goest." (Josh. 1:9). Let all men, young and old, take back the authority that God has given you, and pray without ceasing!

THE PRAYERS OF A RIGHTEOUS MAN

In this day and time men need encouragement like never before. They need to know they are loved and very much needed in this world. They also need Godly wisdom and understanding of the ways of the kingdom of God. Jesus is our supreme example in how to live as holy men of God. He prayed often to the Father, putting His earthly life completely in God's hands. Even though He was very God and man, He looked to the Father for everything. In the same way men must look to the father for everything. The world says you should be macho men, showing how tough you are. But Jesus is calling for men who are strong in spirit, men who are willing to serve and love Him with all their heart, soul, mind, and strength, men who are willing to go to Him in prayer, not leaning on their own mind for understanding, but putting everything in His hands, acknowledging that God is in control of all things, and He it is, who directs our paths. (See Luke 10:27 and Prov. 3:5-6). It is not the physical that God looks at, that's what the world looks at to determine if a man is strong or not. God looks at the heart, what a man is like on the inside. Pumping iron, running, jogging, eating healthy, all may be good for the body, but it doesn't make for a

Glimpses of Grace

healthy soul. The Father wants men who are willing to commune with Him in prayer, seeking His face, seeking His will. "The effectual fervent prayer of a righteous man availeth much." (James 5:16b)

The Word of God says that if any man be in Christ, he is made new, and all the old sinful things in his life are no longer a part of him. He is therefore fit to be used by God for the glory of the kingdom of God. "He hath shewed thee, O man, what is good; and what doth the LORD require of thee, but to do justly, and to love mercy, and to walk humbly with thy God?" (Mic. 6:8). Jesus has given you authority over all the powers of the enemy and power to trample on serpents and scorpions: this is the authority of the believer. You have the victory through our Lord and Savior Jesus Christ, and nothing shall harm you. (See Luke 10:19). Now walk in the authority that God has given you, and the greatest part of this authority is that you can pray and know that God always hears and answers your prayers. "And since we know He hears us when we make our requests, we also know that He will give us what we ask for." (1 John 5:15). Stand strong, you mighty men of God; fight the good fight of faith: you are on the winning side.

GOD WILL SUPPLY

In the Sermon on the Mount, Jesus taught us many things about how to live this life the way God meant for us to live. In Matthew 6:24-34, He teaches us to trust and depend on Him for all that we need in life. We cannot serve God and the deceitfulness of riches and the pleasures of this world. Money and riches certainly can keep our minds on things, and not on God. We become materialistic and lose sight of who God is. "Mammon" becomes our god and the mall our church. When we realize that Jesus is our source for all our needs we don't have to worry about clothes, food, and shelter. God is our Father, and a good father will not leave his children without their physical needs supplied, the necessities of life. If earthly fathers will provide for their children, how much more will God our Father, care for us, His children? He owns the cattle on a thousand hills; all riches come from Him. "Both riches and honor come from You and You reign over all." (1 Chron. 29:12)

When we focus on money and things – possessions, we put them before God and forget about Him. Jesus said it is hard for a rich man to enter into heaven. Why is this so? Because he feels he has all he needs and doesn't need God, the One who has the whole world in His hands. A rich man depends on his riches and possessions to gain whatever happiness he needs in life, not realizing that the mammon is temporal and will pass away. It will not last forever and he certainly cannot take it with him when he leaves this life. Have you ever seen a moving truck being pulled behind a hearse? It's all left behind! The Word of God tells us that the wealth of the wicked is laid up for the just. (See Prov. 13:22). When they leave this earth all they possess and worshiped will be for the children of God, to be used for His kingdom.

So, what is the solution to having all our needs met without falling into the sin of denying God? Make Him the center of all of our efforts. Jesus said, "But seek ye first the kingdom of God, and His righteousness; and all these things shall be added unto you." (Matt. 6:33). Put Him first in your life and focus your mind on having a right relationship with Him; and all these things, these possessions, and necessities of life will be given to you. Philippians 4:19 says, "But my God shall supply all your need according to His riches in glory by Christ Jesus." There is no limit to the riches in the kingdom of God. When we put Him first and His kingdom; doing His will and obeying His Word, He says our eyes have not seen, our ears have not heard, neither can our minds conceive of the things that He has prepared for those who love Him and put their trust in Him (See 1 Cor. 2:9). He loves us and wants us to be totally dependent on Him for everything in our lives; not some things, but everything, because He is the only One who can supply our every need and give us more than enough blessings. He wants the best for His children and if we put Him first in our lives that is exactly what we will have. "Fear not, little flock; for it is the Father's good pleasure to give you the kingdom." (Luke 12:32)

LIVE IN THE TRUTH OF GOD

Jesus is about to end His Sermon on the Mount and is now giving His disciples some last warnings as He is about to send them out into the world. They are now going out as "Ambassadors for Christ," representing Him with the authority He has given them. They will now be living their lives according to the message of the Beatitudes (with "beautiful attitudes") and all that Jesus has taught them in His great Sermon. But He is warning then that, "there are going to be some false prophets out there to try to trip you up." Watch out for them, they are only out there for their own greed and selfishness. And you will know them by the life they live and what they are producing in the lives of others. Paul says that we should, "Try the spirits by the Spirit of God." (1 John 4:1-3). The Spirit of God in me can discern the Spirit of God in someone else, because God's Spirit speaks and reacts to His Spirit. But if the spirit in a person is not of God it shall be revealed by His (God's) Spirit. Just as God's wrath was upon the false prophets in Jeremiah's day, He hasn't changed and feels the same way about false prophets today. When a true prophet speaks, his words come to pass, there is a manifestation of the words he has spoken. A false prophet, on the other hand, tells the people lies, things that they know the people want to hear to make them feel good, so that they will be willing to give up their money when the false prophet calls for an offering.

I was in a church service one time when there was a "prophet" praying for the people. After a time, he called for an offering and had his mind totally on the offering instead of the people coming for prayer. One man went for prayer while the offering was being taken and the "prophet" told the man to come back to another service and then he would pray for him. Jesus says they are like corrupt bad trees that produce bad fruit. We had to have a seemingly beautiful shade tree in our yard cut down because it was rotten at the roots. You would never have known except for the tree surgeon telling us. He also cut down a neighbor's tree across the street from us, and he told me the tree had about fifty snakes in it. It looked good on the outside but was corrupt at the foundation.

We must remember that even though we may not be a prophet, we are constantly speaking into the lives of others. Are we speaking life bearing fruit, fruit that will remain, or are we speaking corrupt fruit that brings death and destruction? Pray that we be real for Jesus in every area of our lives, so that we can bear good fruit, producing souls for the kingdom. The Word of God says, "God is a Spirit: and they that worship Him must worship Him in spirit and in truth." (John 4:24). Watch out for false prophets, inside and out. Live in and speak only the truth of God, in love.

ALL THINGS NEW

"Remember ye not the former things, neither consider the things of old. Behold, I will do a new thing; now it shall spring forth: shall ye not know it? I will even make a way in the wilderness, and rivers in the desert." (Isa. 43:18-19)

What was your life like last year? Were all of your heart's desires fulfilled? Was it better than the year before? Are there things you wish you could have changed; things you didn't accomplish that you wanted to have done before this new year? Are there things you did that you wish you had not done? As we look back over the past year, we all probably have some things we say we "should of, would of, could of… if only." But the past is now the past and we have been blessed with a new day, a new year, a new future, because God has it in HIS plan for us. He says He will do a NEW thing, and we will know it; He is going to unfold the plan He has for us this year. Don't expect this year to be like last year, that is not God's plan. Look for the great and mighty things that God can do in your life, in the life of your loved ones. Don't miss the blessings, stay alert, stay close to Him, and stay in His Word. He has things to say to you and to show you. He has new things He wants you to do as you apply His Word to your life each and every day. Yes, you will still have trials and tribulations, that goes without saying, but you are stronger than you were last year. We grow in grace from year to year as we learn more, and as we understand more of the ways of the kingdom of God. As you read and study the Word of God, you will see what you didn't see last year, and you will understand what you didn't understand the year before. That's because you have grown to be more like Jesus!

All things new!!! That's what the Father is doing; so be ready to move when He says move; be ready to go where He says to go; be ready to speak when He says speak; be ready to do what He says to do. We must be totally involved in His new thing, and in total obedience to His will. "And He that sat upon the throne said, Behold, I make all things new, And He said unto me, Write: for these words are true and faithful. And He said unto me, It is done. I Am Alpha and Omega, the beginning and the end. I will give unto him that is athirst of the fountain of the water of life freely, He that overcometh shall inherit all things; and I will be his God, and he shall be my son." (Rev. 21:5-7)

MARY DIDN'T KNOW

Mary had a baby and she named Him, Jesus. If you are a mother, think about your first born and the fear you may have had in your heart because you didn't know how to handle this new tiny little creature. You had total responsibility to take care of this baby, to nurture him/her, teaching, and guiding in the right direction. You had no idea what raising a child would entail. You had no idea there would be heartache and pain in your life while raising the child. All you could see was a tiny little baby who would certainly need your help, your love, and your care. Imagine what must have been going on in Mary's heart and mind. The Bible says, "She pondered all these things in her heart." "Jesus is here, now, Father; what do I do with Him? How do I raise this Son that You have given me responsibility over?" (See Luke 2:19 & 51). You may be one who is reading this and is pregnant right now with your first born. Are you praying, seeking the Father, asking questions so you will know what to do with your baby; how to raise him/her up in "the nurture and admonition of the Lord?" (See Ephesians 6:4). The Father has all the answers. Mary was not alone in caring for Baby Jesus and as He grew and "increased in wisdom and stature, and in favor with God and man," the Father was with her all the time. The Holy Ghost was there to guide

Glimpses of Grace

and direct her, teaching her what to do, what to say, and how to train Jesus in His early life. Then, at the age of twelve, Jesus let Mary know that He knew why He was here. He knew the work the Father had sent Him to do. Mary didn't know, as she held this precious Gift in her arms, that Jesus would one day be healing the sick, raising the dead, and making blind men see (spiritually and physically). She had no idea how the Father would be working in His life. She did know that He would one day "save His people from their sin," but she did not know how it was going to happen and she was certainly not prepared for Calvary.

As parents, we make plans for our children, we have dreams and aspirations of what we want them to become in life; how we want them to prosper and contribute to the good in this world. But it doesn't always come out that way. The Bible says that man makes plans but God is the One who carries them out. Our plans may not be what God has predestinated for the life of our children. He knows what He wants them to be and do in life. No, Mary didn't know how Jesus' life would play out and we don't know how our children's lives will play out. But we know who has them in His hands and there is power in prayer. As we pray and keep them before the Lord for His will to be done in their lives, we can have the blessed assurance that it will work out for their good. "And we know that all things work together for good to them that love God, to them who are the called according to His purpose." (Rom. 8:28)

JESUS, OUR SAVIOR

Why is it that we celebrate the birth of our Savior only one time during the year? This is an event that we should remember every day of our lives. God Almighty stepped down from His glory and into the flesh of mankind to deliver us from the slavery of sin. What great love! No one loves us that way. He could have come as a great king, but He chose to come as a humble little baby boy, the same way all babies are born into the world, through the womb of a woman. And then Jesus lived His life on earth going through all the temptations and the trials a male child goes through throughout his life. Jesus knew what it was like to be a toddler, a young child, a teen, and a young adult. He is our example in life and we can't say He doesn't understand what we go through. We will never suffer as He did for us. He was hated, rejected, bullied, even by His own brothers and sisters, and He did not deserve any of it. Many times we cause our own pain and suffering, but Jesus didn't do that. This was Emmanuel, "God with us," on His way to the cross, the cross of redemption for all mankind. There was no turning back for Jesus, He came to die and nothing could have made Him change His mind. This was the Father's plan to bring us back to Him. Jesus knowing all things, knew how much He would have to suffer in order to bring us back to the Father, but He was willing to do the Father's will. He said, "Nevertheless, not what I will, but what Thou wilt." (Mark 14:37). It was indeed a long journey for Jesus, but He pulled His strength from the Father as He continuously stayed in contact with Him through prayer. Whatever Jesus did, He was doing only what the Father told Him to do. As we go through this journey of life, we too must keep in constant contact with the Father, pulling our strength from Him. "He is the strength of my life, of whom shall I be afraid?"

There is nothing the Father will not do to get us through every tunnel, over every mountain, through every valley in life to make it to the other side. He wants us to reach the finish line, and with Him on our side we will win, and we will make it "home." We must keep our eyes lifted up unto the hills where our help comes from, knowing that we can do all things through Christ who strengthens us. Jesus made it from the cradle to the cross, and now the ball is in our court. Don't drop it, stay in the game, and keep running to the end. "To him that overcometh will I grant to sit with Me in My throne, even as I also overcame, and Am set down with My Father in His throne." (Rev. 3:21)

DO YOU KNOW HIM?

When Jesus walked the earth the people wanted to know just who He was. Some knew Him to be Joseph's Son, the carpenter. Others knew Him to be Mary's Son out of wedlock, so they thought. Some knew Him to be a good teacher. Others who saw His miracles knew Him to be a miracle worker. But who is He really? God has many names, and Jesus is just one of them. Whatever God's name is, that is who He is and what He does. His names are His attributes. He can be whoever you need Him to be in your life. A refuge in time of trouble, a strong tower when you need a fortress, a healer when your body is sick, or a light when your way is dark and you cannot see. Who is He in your life? Jesus is a way-maker, He can make a way out of no way. He is certainly a miracle worker because He does what no other one can do. Jesus always keeps His promises, He never fails what He says He will do, He always does just that, we can trust Him. Jesus is our Savior and the Lover and Bishop of our souls. He loves us unconditionally. His name means Savior, and He saves us in all kinds of situations and circumstances. We can call upon His name and know that He will hear and answer us, day or night. He is awesome in all His ways and His ways are past finding out. We can't figure Him

Glimpses of Grace

out, and we can't know what He is thinking and what He will do. He says His ways are higher than our ways and His thoughts are higher than our thoughts. There is no way our finite minds can match His infinite mind. He is Jehovah God, King of kings and Lord of lords. He is the Great I Am that I Am.

One day Jesus asked His disciples, "Who do people say the Son of Man is?" They replied, "Some say John the Baptist; others say Elijah; and still others, Jeremiah or one of the prophets." "But what about you?" He asked. "Who do you say I am?" Simon Peter answered, "You are the Messiah, the Son of the living God." Jesus replied, "Blessed are you, Simon son of Jonah, for this was not revealed to you by flesh and blood, but by My Father in heaven." (Matt. 16:13-17 NIV). Who do you say that Jesus is?

A MATTER OF FORGIVENESS

Crucifixion was not uncommon in the Roman Empire. This was the Roman's way of really torturing criminals and putting them to death for crimes they had committed. So here we have our Lord Jesus Christ, hanging on a cursed cross, along with two criminals who were thieves. But Jesus had done no wrong, He didn't deserve to be crucified on a cross. As He hung there suffering excruciating pain, his first mind was on forgiveness. He prayed for his enemies, "Father forgive them; for they know not what they do." (Luke 23:34)

Now we have two criminals, one hanging on either side of Jesus, and I am sure they had heard about all the miracles and the good Jesus had done among the people. They probably had, at some point, been in the crowds that gathered around Jesus as He taught and healed the people. One thief lashes out at Jesus in desperation, saying, if You really are who You say You are, "save Yourself and us." (Luke 23:39). And the other one rebukes that thief and asks Jesus to remember him when He comes into His kingdom. Notice one says, "If" and the other one says, "When." There was no doubt in that thief's mind that Jesus was who He said He was. He had the fear of God in his heart and the Holy Spirit revealed to him who Jesus was; just as the Holy Ghost did for Peter. (See Matt. 16:16). That thief had faith in Jesus, and Jesus had taught over and over again that it was faith that moved the hand of God. "According to your faith be it unto you." (Matt. 9:29). So, Jesus' reply to the thief was an eternal life-giving word, "Verily, I say unto thee, to day thou shalt be with Me in paradise." (Luke 23:43). It was a word of forgiveness.

Jesus did not go back to the Father empty handed. The thief was His first convert, washed in His blood. He didn't have time to be baptized, and he didn't have time to receive the baptism of the Holy Ghost and speaking in tongues, but he made it in. He was escorted by the Lord Jesus Christ, Himself, and presented to the Father by Him. Jesus said the first shall be last and the last shall be first. So many people have been in the "way" for years, working their fingers to the bone, thinking they are doing what Jesus wants them to do and they will hear, *"Depart from Me, I never knew you."* (See Matt. 7:23). Could it be a heart problem? What is the motive behind all of the work? The thief had no hidden agenda. He came just as he was, nothing fixed up trying to impress Jesus. God wants from us a broken and contrite heart. He wants repentance with true humility, just like that thief, hanging there on the cross. He requires our complete trust in Him.

"It is not the will of God that any should perish, but that all should come to repentance." (2 Peter 3:9). "Jesus died for the whole world, He came not to condemn the world, but that the world through Him might be saved." (John 3:17). The thief was a part of the world that Jesus came to save. We cannot pick and choose who we will witness to or who we will tell about the good news of the Gospel. Our duty is to bring souls to Jesus no matter what it takes to get it done; the unlovely, the unkind, the unforgivable, the down and outers, the smelly drunkard, the dirty drug addict, and yes, the lying thief. Jesus' forgiveness reaches out to all of them; red, yellow, brown, black, white, Jew, and gentile; the whole world.

If we expect God to wipe our slate clean, we will have to free others with the same forgiveness that Jesus extended on the cross to that dying thief. Jesus forgave and interceded for His accusers. True forgiveness does not remember the bad or the way the wrong was done. True forgiveness is not judgmental. Remember, we will be judged by the same measuring stick that we use to judge. When we do not release others y forgiving them, we hurt ourselves. We actually place ourselves in bondage and the blessings of God are unable to truly flow in our lives because there is a blockage. Jesus did not think about all the wrong the thief had done, He looked at his repentant heart and covered him in His blood, and released him from his sins. "For if ye forgive men their trespasses, your heavenly Father will also forgive you: But if ye forgive not men their trespasses, neither will you Father forgive your trespasses." (Matt. 6:14-15)

AGAINST ALL ODDS

"The LORD is my light and my salvation; whom shall I fear? The LORD is the strength of my life; of whom shall I be afraid?" (Ps. 27:1)

When God has a mission for us and wants to move us to another level, He moves us out of our comfort zone, and we may find that we have to fight some tough battles. Our enemy doesn't care how he takes us out as long as he thinks he's going to win. But in the midst of the battle God sends us help. No enemy we face is too big for God to handle.

How many of you know that God always has a plan? He knows just how He is going to help us win the battle, all He asks is that we trust Him and let Him do it His way. We can't pick and choose who we want to teach and train us. God is the One who does the choosing, it's His plan and He knows just how to work it out. There are things God has us go through and we may feel it is senseless and meaningless. *"Why do I have to follow all these rules, it doesn't take all of this to be what I want to be; this teacher doesn't know as much as I know"*; and all the time, we are talking about the Holy Ghost, whom God has sent

Glimpses of Grace

to help us. We have to learn how to come down and be humble under the leadership of our Teacher; we have to get it on the inside before it can be manifested on the outside. The Holy Ghost has to teach us the Beatitudes (beautiful attitudes) recorded in Matthew 5th chapter, before they can be manifested in our lives as the "Fruit of the Spirit" in Galatians 5th chapter. And all the time God is working things out for our good!!! He is moving us up to another level.

We don't have to fear no matter how hard the test may seem. Whether it is sickness, lack of finances, broken relationships, or wayward children, the same Holy Ghost is with us to help us. When we are most weak, God shows Himself strong on our behalf. All He wants is for us to trust Him. The Holy Spirt will teach us techniques the enemy can't handle. "We are more than conquerors, through Him that loved us." (Rom. 8:37). "Through God we shall do valiantly, for He it is that shall tread down our enemies." (Ps. 108:13). Against all odds, He will make us to come out victoriously! God fully equips us for the battles we have to face. He lets us fight them or He fights them for us; either way, we win!

ARE YOU POT-BOUND?

> "Blessed is the man that trusteth in the LORD, and whose hope the LORD is. For he shall be as a tree planted by the waters, and that spreadeth out her roots by the river, and shall not see when heat cometh, but her leaf shall be green; and shall not be careful in the year of drought, neither shall cease from yielding fruit." (Jer. 17:7-8)

Those of you who know anything about having house plants probably know what it means for a plant to be "pot-bound." You may have a plant that you started from a tiny shoot or from another plant. In time, that plant starts to grow and becomes too large for the small pot that it is in. The roots of the plant have grown very long and have to curl up in a tight mass because they have no room to grow. The plant begins to lose its brightness, the leaves lose their dark green color and frequently turn yellow and fall off the plant. The plant has become pot-bound. No matter how much you water it and care for it, it still doesn't grow as it did before it became pot-bound. I had a plant such as that, the roots were even exposed above the soil and the soil seemed to be diminishing. I knew the plant had

Glimpses of Grace

to be repotted because its roots had no room to continue to grow. It didn't produce the beautiful red flowers like it used to, and the leaves were frequently falling and branches becoming bare. After I replanted it in a larger pot and moved it to a larger space where it could spread with freedom to grow, it really prospered.

Our lives are like that plant. God wants to give us eagle wings so we can grow and fly and be free from bondage. Anxiety, fear, and unbelief in our life can make us pot-bound. We've got to trust God and know, without a shadow of a doubt, that He knows what He is doing and that He is in control of our life. Sickness can make us pot-bound so we cannot do the work of the Lord. Instead of being bound up and tangled up with Jesus, we are focusing on our infirmities. The beauty of Jesus cannot be seen in our life because we are pot-bound with no room to spread. We cannot function to our full capacity. The flower of our life cannot bloom because we have no room for our roots to spread and receive the oxygen needed to maintain life. The "water of the Word" cannot reach its mark to give proper nourishment so our life can flourish and show forth the glory of the Lord. Jabez prayed that God would enlarge his border, and God answered his prayer. (See 1 Chron. 4:10)

We need to pray that same prayer and allow the Holy Spirit to straighten out our roots and give us more room to grow. If we allow Him, He will transplant us and move us to a larger place, a better environment where we can

Glimpses of Grace

grow and be a blessing to those around us. God will bring people into our life who need a word of encouragement, who need someone who can get a prayer through, who need a listening ear and a caring heart. But we cannot be that someone if we are pot-bound and our roots tangled up with fear, unbelief, and the cares of this world. God wants to put us in a large place so He can use us and get the glory out of our life. Our purpose is to glorify Him! Allow the Holy Spirit to shake out those roots and bring you into a large place where the life force of Jesus can water those roots; and then you will grow more beautifully for the glory of God's kingdom. "If the Son therefore shall make you free, ye shall be free indeed." (John 8:36)

LOOK UP

The Word of God tells us that Jesus is coming soon. The signs of the time tell us that He is soon to come. In the Bible in Matthew 24th chapter and Luke 21st chapter, it tells us what to look for in the end time. "And then shall they see the Son of man coming in a cloud with power and great glory. And when these things begin to come to pass, then look up, and lift up your heads; for your redemption draweth nigh." (Luke 21:27; 28). The Lord Jesus Christ wants us to be ready for His soon coming. No one knows the day nor the hour, but if we follow the Word of God, stay tuned to the Holy Spirit, and lean not on our own understanding, if we acknowledge God in everything we say and do, allowing Him to direct our path, we can be ready. Jesus said He is coming as a "thief in the night." You don't want to be caught off guard. We have to be on our posts day and night, no time out for bad behavior. When things are going well, and we can see God's blessing in our life, and even when it looks like everything is falling apart, we have to be on guard. Jesus said, "Occupy until I come." (See Luke 19:13). He has given us talents to be used for His glory. We can't be sitting around in our comfort zone doing nothing. "*Occupy*" is an action word. We must be busy about the Father's business, doing what He has purposed for us to do, and don't stop until Jesus comes. (See Luke 19:12-27). He expects us to be doing the *"greater works"* when He comes back: healing the sick, raising the dead, bringing souls into His kingdom, teaching and preaching His Word, helping the poor and needy, going to hospitals and nursing homes, and taking songs and the Word of God to build up and strengthen the weak.

We've got to keep oil in our lamps and keep them burning until the Bridegroom comes for His bride. Remember the story of the ten virgins; five wise and five foolish? (See Matt. 25:1-13). Those wise virgins knew they had to have oil in those lamps to keep them burning, or they would not have been ready to meet the Bridegroom. The foolish virgins had no oil and tried to get some at the last minute, but they were too late. If you have no oil and your lamp goes out, how can you see to do the work of the Lord? "Night is coming when no man can work." (John 9:4)

Have you ever started out on a trip and realized your gas tank was almost on empty? You know it is urgent that you get some gas, but you make a few stops along the way before you get to the gas station; all the time using up the little bit of gas you had in the beginning. Then, the tank is empty, the car stops, and you can't go anywhere until you get a refill. While we are waiting for Jesus' return, we still have work to do. Therefore, we have to keep our gas tank full. There are souls to be saved, captives to be set free, bodies to be healed, souls to be strengthened and

Glimpses of Grace

encouraged, and a lot of love to be given out. We can't do this if our tanks are running on "empty." We are going to need a refilling regularly. We must stay in the Word of God in order to get direction, comfort, and strength. We have to stay in communion with God our Father through constant and consistent prayer, and we must fellowship with the body of Christ so we can strengthen and encourage each other and be fed by the Word of God through His pastors and teachers.

Stay on spiritual tiptoes looking for the appearing of our Lord and Savior Jesus Christ. Occupy until He comes, with your gas tank full, because you still have a lot of errands to run, using the talents God has given you, being fruitful and productive in bringing souls into the kingdom. Live every day as though you know it to be your last day on earth, and as though you know Jesus is coming today. "Looking for that blessed hope, and the glorious appearing of the great God and our Savior Jesus Christ." (Titus 2:13)

ARE YOU TURNING YOUR WORLD UPSIDE DOWN?

When we pray in the power of the Holy Ghost, which is that dynamite explosive power, everything is affected around us. First of all, it blows away things on the inside of us and then it explodes out of us and touches everything around us. The Holy Ghost is the One who enables us to pray in the will of the Father. When we pray in the Spirit we are praying above that which we understand because we are praying with the mind of Christ, who is equal with the Father, because Jesus and the Father are one. But the Father says that His ways are not our ways neither are His thoughts our thoughts, for as the heaven is higher than the earth so are His ways higher than our ways and His thoughts higher than our thoughts. Don't try to figure God out, just pray whatever the Holy Spirit leads you to pray. When Jesus' disciples came to Him and asked Him to teach them how to pray, Jesus told them to say, "Our Father, Which art in heaven, Hallowed be Thy Name." This is the model prayer that Jesus taught His disciples to say when they pray. The Lord's Prayer is John 17, the prayer Jesus prayed just before He went to the Garden of Gethsemane.

Glimpses of Grace

This prayer that Jesus taught His disciples to pray is power packed! In spreading the Gospel of Jesus Christ, the disciples preached and prayed, and the Scriptures say in Acts 17:6, "These have turned the world upside down." Paul and Silas were preaching up a storm in Thessalonica and I'm sure they were also praying up a storm, and Paul, having been taught by Jesus while in the desert, I'm sure was also taught how to pray even as Jesus taught the disciples. Now, if their prayers were turning the world upside down, shouldn't we, too, be turning the world upside down with our prayers? I remember my former pastor, who lived to be 103 years old, asked me one day if I was turning my world upside down with this prayer. She taught me how we can take any person, place, or thing we are praying for, and put them in the middle of this prayer, and know without a shadow of a doubt that God is going to answer because we are praying the way He taught us to pray. We can pray, "Thy kingdom come, Thy will be done in my husband; my brother; my sister; my children; because in Your kingdom, Father, there is salvation, healing, peace, deliverance…" Pray whatever you need God's kingdom to come in, and His will to be done in. But in order for this prayer to be effective as we intercede, it must first be effective in our own life. It's not just something we learned by heart as children and now we run through it not even realizing what we are praying. Take time to stop at each phrase and meditate on what you are praying, allow the Holy Spirit to speak to you as

Glimpses of Grace

you pray these words, and you will feel the power of God permeating in every word. Then, your effective prayers will turn your world upside down. "Father, I thank You that You have heard me. I know that You always hear Me." (John 11:42)

EFFECTUAL PRAYERS

I think we underestimate the power of prayer. Jesus did a lot of praying as He walked this earth and His disciples realized the power He walked in because they often saw and heard Him pray. That is why they asked Him to teach them how to pray. When they could not cast out the devil from the young man, Jesus told them some things only come out by prayer and fasting. They didn't forget what Jesus taught them, and as we read in the Book of Acts (the Acts of the Holy Ghost through the disciples), they were turning their world upside down. When Jesus gave them His guideline for prayer (See Matt. 6:9-15), they took it and ran with it, they lived it, they believed it, and they shared it. How are we doing?

We cannot pray, "***Our,***" if our faith has no room for others and their needs. We cannot pray, "***Father***," if we do not demonstrate this relationship to God in our daily living. We cannot pray, "***Who Art in Heaven***," if all of our interests and pursuits are in earthy things and we are not seeking "those things above." We cannot pray, "***Hallowed be Thy Name***," if I we are not striving for God's help to be holy. If we are not walking in the holiness of God, acknowledging that He is Holy, we cannot pray for His holiness to be in any situation. We cannot pray, "***Thy Kingdom Come***," if we are not willing to accept God's rule for our life. We cannot pray, "**Thy Will be Done**," if we are unwilling or resentful of having it in our life or if we want to lean unto our own understanding and walk in our own way. After Satan was cast out of heaven, there is no one up there wanting to do their own thing. Nothing but God's will is being done! We cannot pray, "**In Earth as it is in Heaven**," unless we are truly ready to give ourselves to God's service here and now, and we are willing to allow Him to do what He wants to do in these "earthen vessels." We cannot pray, "**Give us This Day Our Daily Bread**," if we are not eating the Bread as Jesus commanded, but are rejecting Jesus, who is the Bread of Life, or if we are withholding from our neighbor the Bread we receive. We cannot pray, "**Forgive Us Our Trespasses as We Forgive Those Who Trespass Against Us**," if we continue to harbor a grudge against anyone and refuse to forgive them. Jesus said His Father will not forgive us if we don't forgive others. We cannot pray, "**Lead Us Not Into Temptation**," if we deliberately choose to remain or put ourselves in a situation where we are likely to be tempted. We can't go knocking on the devil's door and ask God to lead us not into temptation. We cannot pray, "**But Deliver Us From Evil (or The Evil One)**," if we are not prepared to fight the battle having on the Whole Armor of God. We must keep it on at all times, from head to toe (See Eph. 6:10-18). We cannot pray, "**For Thine is the Kingdom**," if we are unwilling to obey the King. We cannot pray, "**And the Power and the Glory**," if we are seeking power for ourselves and our own glory. We cannot pray, "***Forever***," if we are too anxious about each day's affairs and refuse to lay our burdens down, trusting that all power is in God's hands and there is nothing He cannot do. We cannot pray, "***Amen***," unless we honestly say, "Not my will, but Thy will be done, so let it be."

When we pray this prayer the way Jesus meant for it to be prayed, first working in us, then we can truly turn the world upside down as we place persons, places, and things in the midst of this prayer and ***expect*** God to do great and mighty things in the lives of others, as He honors His Word, knowing that, "..***The effectual fervent prayer of a righteous man availeth much***." (James 5:16b)

CHANGED FROM THE INSIDE OUT

God has provided an inheritance for all of us, but we haven't experienced it because of our lack of understanding about meekness. When we think of meekness we think humble, lowly, and gentle. We might even think being meek is being weak. Actually, meekness is "controlled power." Our Lord Jesus Christ called Himself meek and He certainly was not weak at all. He also said that "all power in heaven and earth belonged to Him." So, we know He was not weak. As we learn to control the power that is within us, we shall inherit all that God has planned for us. We have so much power that we don't even realize it, and it starts in our minds. You see why Satan tries to attack our minds? He knows we have power in our minds. He cannot read our minds, but he knows our mind is powerful. The Word of God says, "For who has known the mind of the Lord, that he man instruct Him? But we have the mind of Christ." (I Cor. 2:16). The Holy Spirit takes the things of Jesus and shows them to us. He reveals to us what is in Jesus' mind. How blessed we are!

Now we have to control our thinking. It's already in us!!! What is in us? The power to change our circumstances. The change comes from the inside out. "As a man thinketh in his heart, so is he." (See Prov. 23:7). Thoughts produce habits (there are good habits and bad habits); habits produce actions that effect our decisions; actions produce character; and character produces our destiny. God's Word has no progress in us because of the way we think. We have to renew our minds, be transformed by the renewing of our minds, and change the way we think. Look at this example: When Jesus was on the ship with His disciples, He was at perfect peace, asleep when the storm arose. His disciples were afraid and thinking they were going to die. They needed to change their way of thinking. Jesus had peace on the inside so He could sleep in the midst of the storm. He had peace on the inside so He could speak to the storm and make it be still. Do you realize that Jesus' actions were always the opposite of what His disciples thought He would do? They didn't think the way He did. When Lazarus died Jesus did the opposite of what His disciples thought He would do. He didn't go right away. When He went to Jerusalem to die, His disciples told Him not to go, Jesus did the opposite. Having the mind of Christ makes all the difference in the world. Do you realize that we have that same power if we walk in the Spirit and not in the flesh. We can still the storms in our lives, but we have to get rid of the wrong thinking that feeds our souls, and when we do, it will affect everything in our lives; our homes, our marriage, our children, our jobs, our finances; every area of our lives. Jesus has given us power over all the powers of the enemy. We can tread on serpents and scorpions. We are more than conquerors. So, who's afraid of the big bad wolf? A storm, "Peace be still!," a mountain, "Move!" We must plead the blood of Jesus over our minds and walk in the meekness of our Lord and Savior Jesus Christ, and receive the promise of God to inherit the earth. "Blessed are the meek: for they shall inherit the earth." (Matt. 5:5)

A NEW CREATURE IN CHRIST

When we give our life to Jesus, He makes all things new. We just need to follow His lead. It is not something we can conqueror overnight. We have to get into the habit of knowing Jesus is our example. We have to deal with the thoughts that do not line up with the Word of God. Jesus said, "Come unto Me, all ye that labor and are heavy laden, and I will give you rest. Take My yoke upon you, and learn of (from) Me; for I am meek and lowly in heart: and ye shall find rest unto your souls. For My yoke is easy, and My burden is light." (Matt. 11:28-30). These wrong thoughts are the way the devil gains access to our lives. We have to put up a roadblock to keep the devil from gaining access and that roadblock is the Word of God. Paul says we are to be transformed by the renewing of our minds, so that we may understand what is the good and perfect will of God. (See Rom. 12:2). We have to get into the habit of saying what God says about us in every situation. When you feel you have lost the battle and can't fight any more, God says, "I am more than a conqueror." When your body is sick and the doctor says you can't get well, God says, "I am healed. I shall not die but live and declare the works of the Lord." When it seems that all hell is breaking out in your family and home, God says, "I shall be saved and my house." God says, "Greater is He Who is in you than he who is in the world." God says, "I am the head and not the tail." God says, "I am above and not beneath."

We have to bring into captivity every thought to the obedience of Christ. Pull down every stronghold and every thought that is against what we know about God. We have read His Word, we know what it says, and we have even seen God work in the past in our lives and in the lives of others. We have to continuously feed on the Word of God and act on His Word in order to block the devil's access to our minds. If it doesn't line up with the Word of God, get rid of it immediately! "Finally, brethren, whatsoever things are true, whatsoever things are honest, whatsoever things are just, whatsoever things are pure, whatsoever things are lovely, whatsoever things are of good report; if there be any virtue, and if there be any praise, think on these things." (Phil. 4:8). Keep putting into practice all you have received and learned, and all you have heard and seen God do. Activate the "controlled power" that is on the inside and receive the inheritance God has already given you. Form good habits in your mind and be changed from the inside out. Walk in the spirit of meekness and you shall inherit the earth, it's all through Jesus Christ our Lord. "If ye then be risen with Christ, seek those things which are above, where Christ sitteth on the right hand of God. Set your affection on things above, not on things on the earth." (Col. 3:1-2)

CHERISH THE MOMENT

"This is the day which the LORD hath made; we will rejoice and be glad in it." (Ps. 118:24).

Do we feel this way about every day that God has chosen to awaken us and give us life? We all have or have had days when we wish we could just cover our heads and let it pass, but God has a plan and purpose for each day of our lives. He wakes us up so we can invite Him in with His new mercies and grace for the day. David prayed to God, "Cause me to hear Thy loving-kindness in the morning; for in Thee do I trust: cause me to know the way wherein I should walk; for I lift up my soul unto Thee." (Ps. 143:8)

When you really think about it, life is very short. Look how fast our children grow up and are gone away from home. You look back and wonder where the time went. Some people don't want to acknowledge their birthday each year because it reminds them that time is passing by. Yes, time is passing by, and we should cherish each moment we have on this earth, each moment we have with our families, each moment we are able to make a difference in someone's life, and each moment we have to give God glory and praise, the One who gives us life, health, and strength. When God gives you another day, be thankful and ask Him what He wants you to do this day; what plans does He have for you? It is His day, He made it but He didn't feel it to be complete without you and me. What an amazing God we serve! Don't take your time for granted because each moment is strategically planned by God. Live in the moment of time you have right now. "LORD, make me to know mine end, and the measure of my days, what it is; that I may know how frail I am." (Ps. 39:4). Don't waste the precious moments with meaningless things in this life. Take time to smell the roses and be thankful for the dawning of a brand new day. This is the day God has given you to trust Him, lean on Him, seek Him, and depend on Him to get you through, no matter what storms may come your way. Cherish the moments when you can feel Him very close to you. "So teach us to number our days, that we may apply our hearts unto wisdom." (Ps. 90:12). Time is passing on.

BE STRONG IN THE LORD

One of the synonyms for "STRONG" is, "POWERFUL." To be strong is to be able to move heavy weights or tasks that are physically demanding. It also means to be able to withstand great force or pressure, to be indestructible, secure, and well-fortified. Just imagine all this possible in the natural. Now think about being "strong in the Lord!" Wow!!! That means having unlimited strength to do great feats, because God is all powerful, and almighty. There is no one greater than He. David realized this when he wrote in Psalm 27:1, "The LORD is my light and my salvation; whom shall I fear? The LORD is the strength of my life; of whom shall I be afraid?" David proved what it means to be strong in the Lord when he went out against the giant Goliath, with just five smooth stones and a sling. He let Goliath know that he was coming against him, "..in the Name of the LORD Almighty, the God of the armies of Israel." We can move the giants in our lives by going against them in the name of the Lord, because greater is He who is in us than he that is in this world. We have all power through our Lord and Savior Jesus Christ. "The Name of the LORD is a strong tower, the righteous man runs into it and is safe." (Prov. 18:10). David ran toward the enemy, not away from him. He remembered how the

Lord had helped him to defeat the lion and the bear. We don't have to be afraid and run from the enemy, God is the One who fights our battles. In Him we can find all the strength we need to stand strong. Has He ever helped you in the past to defeat the enemy? Well, He is the same yesterday, today, and forever, He hasn't changed and will never change. He helped you before and He will help you now, no matter what you may be going through, just trust Him. The Word of God says that through Him we shall do valiantly, that He is the One who teaches our hands to war and our fingers to fight. We have unlimited power in the Mighty name of the Lord. Jesus said that whatever we ask the Father in His name (Jesus) we shall receive. Stand on your faith as David did, knowing that nothing is impossible with God. God says, "Behold, I Am the LORD, the God of all flesh: is there anything too hard for me?" (Jer. 32:27). Our answer should be, "NO, LORD, there is nothing too hard for You!" "Finally, my brethren, be strong in the Lord, and in the power of His might." (Eph. 6:10)

CLUTTER IN THE PRAYER CLOSET

One day while sitting in my study, which was also my prayer closet, I looked around the room at the different piles of papers, some of which needed to be filed in the file cabinet, some needed to be put into their proper binders, and some just needed to be thrown away. I felt there was such clutter in my prayer closet. At that time, the Holy Ghost spoke to me about the clutter we bring to our prayer closet. Our minds are not focused on God, but on all the cares and worries around us; on the things we need to do as soon as we finish our prayer time; the errands we must run; the dinner we have to prepare; picking our children and grandchildren up from school; who we need to call, etc., etc.

Have you ever tried to make a phone call and you get a message that says, *"All circuits are busy, please try your call later.?"* Can you imagine God trying to get through to us and because of the clutter in our prayer closet, He can't get connected with us? No matter how many people are calling on God we will never hear that message from His phone line. His line is always open and clear for us to get through, but it is on our end that the clutter keeps us from getting through to God. We must clean out the prayer closet, get rid of the junk, file what needs to be filed, and only take it out when you need it. Put other things in their proper places so you will be able to concentrate on God and commune with Him. God wants us to come into our prayer closet with a clear line, and an open mind. Just come in and meet Him there. Remember how it was when you were in love and your loved one came to see you? You weren't thinking about what time they had to leave or what you had to do next, you were only thinking about being with that one and you didn't care what time they left.

I remember my dad would call downstairs, after he felt it was late enough for my loved one to go home, "Bobbi!," and I would answer, "Yes, Sir?" He would ask, "What time is it?" Now, he already knew what time it was, but he wanted me to know that it was time to send Robert home, and for me to go to bed. I wasn't looking at the clock. Who cared what time it was? In that same way, Jesus is the lover of our soul and wants to spend quality time with us. We owe Him that much and more because we are in His debt. He loves us and wants us to come to Him because we love Him and want to be with Him and spend time with Him.

So, let's get the clutter out of our prayer closet and come with our lines cleared and ready to receive whatever God wants to give us for that moment. How can we receive anything if our "circuits are busy?" God can't even get through to tell us how much He loves us. We can't hear His instructions for us and know how and when to move to do His will. The clutter starts in our minds, and it can become overwhelming if we don't get it cleaned out. Even in our ministries, they can get to a point where they become a clutter in our prayer closet. The things that clutter may not be something bad, but if it takes your focus off of God and fellowship with Him, it becomes a clutter. When we allow the Holy Spirit to take control, He will help us to get and keep our priorities straight, with Jesus first. "Put God first and you will never be last." (See Prov. 16:3). We say it with our mouths that God is first, but does our life show it? Do we acknowledge Him first thing in the morning in our prayer closet? Do we acknowledge Him in everything throughout the day? Charles H. Spurgeon said, *"A day hemmed in with prayer is least likely to unravel."* Jesus said, "Love the Lord your God with all your heart and with all your soul and with all your mind and with all your strength." (Mark 12:30). Get rid of the clutter in your prayer closet.

CONSECRATED TO GOD

Consecration is the only way we can live a victorious life in this world. God offers us salvation and baptism in the Holy Ghost, but "*consecration*" means we offer ourselves back to God. Holiness comes after salvation. God commands us to be holy because He is holy. (See 1 Pet. 1:16). Everything we have and are belongs to God and He is waiting for us to offer it back to Him. Jesus Christ gave up the ultimate of His glory for us and we ought to be willing to abandon all for Him; because we love Him. Consecration aims to serve and please God, for His glory and honor. "I beseech you therefore, brethren, by the mercies of God, that ye present your bodies a living sacrifice, holy, acceptable unto God, which is your reasonable service." (Eph. 12:1)

The primary work of the Holy Ghost is not to make you speak in tongues, but to help you live a holy and separated life in this world. "Wherefore come out from among them, and be ye separate, saith the Lord, and touch not the unclean thing; and I will receive you, And will be a Father unto you, and ye shall be my sons and daughters, saith the Lord Almighty." (11 Cor. 6:17-18). We cannot take on the things of this world, conforming to the evil ways of mankind and call ourselves holy and consecrated to God. It is unacceptable to a Holy God. There are things we tolerate

Glimpses of Grace

today, which would never have been mentioned in the church twenty-five or fifty years ago. We look at evil and call it good, and we look at good and call it evil. Anything goes. We no longer measure ourselves according to the Word of God. Holiness is obeying and imitating God.

We must allow the Holy Spirit to have full reign in our innermost being so we can be fit for the Master's use. You can't be unfaithful to your spouse and say you are living holy. You can't be sleeping around or even looking at the opposite sex, lusting in your heart, and say you are living holy. Holiness is keeping God's laws and taking God's side against sin. No matter what the government legislates; abortions, gay rights, men and women marrying the same sex; all of this is an abomination to our Holy God. We have become so absorbed with self, and this has kept us from living holy; we have our own agendas and ideas about being consecrated to our heavenly Father. It takes time and practice to be totally dedicated to God, and we are too busy. We do a lot of work in the church, thinking that it will make us holy. Wrong! If we are too busy to pray, or to read and study God's Word, we are too busy. "Follow peace with all men, and holiness, without which no man shall see the Lord." (Heb. 12:14). Just as Jesus gave Himself totally and completely for us, let us do likewise, withholding nothing of ourselves, that we may be used by God for His glory and honor; totally committed. "Then Joshua said to the people, 'Consecrate yourselves, for tomorrow the LORD will do wonders among you.'" (Josh. 3:5)

EFFECTIVE ON THE BATTLEFIELD

In these last days, all the children of God are in a battle for our lives. Our arch enemy, Satan, is doing all he can do kill, steal, and destroy everything in our lives. We must be on our guard at all times and recognize him when he comes sniffing around. He is subtle, a deceiver, sneaky, and very cunning. Every day we must put on the "Whole armor of God," from the crown of our heads to the souls of our feet, to the tips of our fingers and toes; leaving nothing unprotected or unguarded. (See Eph. 6:10-20). God has given us power over all the powers of the enemy and we don't have to be afraid of him, but know that he can sneak in and overtake us if we leave a door open for him to get in. Get rid of everything in your life that is not pleasing to God: every relationship, every attitude, every habit, and very hidden sin and secret fault we think no one knows about.

In order to be effective on the battlefield of life we must go through boot camp training. Every branch of the military sends its recruits to boot camp. In boot camp they learn discipline, how to follow rules and regulations, how to be humble and to submit to those in authority over them, how to fight with the weapons they are given, and how to know which weapons will be most effective in a given

Glimpses of Grace

situation. In our Christian walk our boot camp training comes from the Holy Spirit and our training manual is the written Word of God. We must do all that it requires of us in order to be strong in battle, enabling us to withstand every test. The Word of God teaches us how to use our weapons of warfare. Every instruction is vital to us winning in every fight. The Holy Ghost is our Drill Instructor and we must humbly submit totally to Him. Listen and do whatever He tells us. Our Commander-in-Chief, Almighty God, tells the Holy Ghost how to direct and guide us in every situation. God gives Him the plans and strategies to give to us. All we have to do is follow His direction and we will not fail.

Some recruits do fail in boot camp. They resist the training, the discipline, and the submission, and they become dropouts. Remember, I said the enemy can get in if we leave a door open for him to enter. That door can be pride of life, feeling we don't need anyone to tell us anything, we know it all, we want it all, we can do it all. Pride is what got our enemy, Satan, thrown out of heaven. He wanted to be like God in heaven. We must be submissive to the will of God, and He will give us the victory in every battle; but without Him we can do nothing. "For though we walk in the flesh, we do not war after the flesh: (For the weapons of our warfare are not carnal, but mighty through God to the pulling down of strongholds;) Casting down imaginations, and every high thing that exalteth itself against the knowledge of God, and bringing into captivity every thought to the obedience of Christ;" (II Cor. 10:3-5)

DETOUR AHEAD

Have you ever been traveling on a certain route, knowing where you were going, when all of a sudden you see police cars blocking the road so you can't continue on that route? This recently happened to me, at night, on a street I travel several times a week, but the surrounding area was unfamiliar to me. I am one who can really get turned around at night even in a familiar place, and even when there is no detour. Alright, I can't go straight, so which way do I go, left or right? I see drivers turning left, so I follow. I follow one driver in particular, who seems to know which way to go. He stops at a dead end and turns left, then another dead end. I finally realized he didn't know where he was going either. After going in wrong directions, having to make U-turns, trying to find my own way, I finally heard the Holy Spirit, who is my Guide, saying, "Turn on your GPS." I had no problem after that. Thank God for that still, small voice. "Whether you turn to the right or to the left, your ears will hear a voice behind you, saying, "This is the way; walk in it." (Isa. 30:21 NIV)

We will find there are many detours in life and most of the time they come unexpectedly. It could be the loss of a loved one, the loss of your job, a devastating sickness, or a broken relationship, and you realize you can't stay on the route you are traveling. No matter what turn you have to make, make sure you are following the right driver. Don't be distracted by following those who seem to know where they are going and are really leading you down the wrong road. God has His reasons for allowing these detours in our lives, to strengthen our faith in Him, and to keep us focused on Him. He knows the end from the beginning, and He knows which is the best route for us to take. We may not know where the detour will take us, but we must trust the Holy Spirit to guide us through safely so we can continue to travel to our destination. It is when we feel we have to take matters into our own hands that we lose our way and waste time trying to get back on track.

Stay connected, turn on your "GPS" (God's Protecting Spirit), and trust Him, follow His lead and He will surely get you to your destination in good form. "Trust in the LORD with all thine heart; and lean not unto thine own understanding. In all thy ways acknowledge Hm, and He shall direct thy paths." (Prov. 3:5-6)

DON'T BYPASS YOUR PIT STOP

Many of us enjoy watching the Olympics, and we find that in most of the events the athletes are racing against time and trying to be the first to win. It takes a lot of hard discipline and training to compete in the Olympics. The Word of God indicates that our Christian walk is like being in a race, and that if we accept the discipline and training, we will be better equipped to run the race to the finish line. This is what is written in Hebrews 12:5-8, and 11-13, the New Living Translation, "And have you entirely forgotten the encouraging words God spoke to you, His children? He said, "My child, don't ignore it when the Lord disciplines you, and don't be discouraged when He corrects you. For the Lord disciplines those He loves, and He punishes those He accepts as His children." As you endure this divine discipline, remember that God is treating you as His own child. Whoever heard of a child who was never disciplined? If God doesn't discipline you as He does all of His children, it means you are illegitimate and are not really His child after all. No discipline is enjoyable while it is happening – it is painful! But afterward there will be a quiet harvest of right living for those who trained in this way. So, take a grip with your tired hands and stand firm on your shaky legs. Mark out a straight path for your feet. Then those who follow you, though they are weak and lame, will not stumble and fall but will become strong.

We have to do what it takes to run this race we are in and reach the finish line. We are not thinking about running on foot but driving a racecar. Picture yourself in the Olympics driving a racecar. (The Lord is moving faster in these "end times" and we need to speed up in order to keep up with Him.) You take off at the sound of the gun (that's the Holy Spirit telling you to take off). Everything is going well, and you are in a good position in the race. You turn your head for a split second to look at the people in the stands; you lose focus, and miss a fast approaching curve. Having lost control, you tap the wall and blow a tire. You've got to make a fast pit stop! Everyone in the race has a pit stop. Remember, everyone in your pit stop is there to help you; they are cheering you on to the end. If you keep on going and bypass the pit stop, you will never be able to finish the race. At that pit stop there are four people on your team waiting to assist you (God the Father, Jesus the Word of God, the Holy Spirit the power of God, and your Guardian Angel). They move with lightning speed to replace the tire and get you back in the race. You are back on the track speeding up to a good position, again. You are doing fine, when suddenly a stone pops up out of nowhere, and cracks your windshield. This impairs your vision so you have to make another fast pit stop. Your team is on the ball; they have just what you need, a new windshield. They replace it with lightning speed and get you back on the track in record time. You make it around the track, completing all of your laps and make it across the finish line.

In this race of life if you miss the mark, if distractions and obstacles get in your way, please don't bypass the pit stop. The Holy Ghost is waiting to give you the grace you need and get you back on track. Accept the Father's discipline. Repent, and ask for God's forgiveness, know that you receive it and keep on going in the race, because it isn't over until God says it's over. "Great and marvelous are Thy works, Lord God Almighty; just and true are Thy ways, Thou King of saints." (Rev. 15:3b)

DON'T BYPASS YOUR PIT STOP (2)

In this race called life, we find that we have to keep going if we are going to finish the race. We can't let our circumstances prevent us from "pressing towards the mark for the prize of the high calling of God in Christ Jesus." (See Phil, 3:14). Life happens, it is inevitable; that's why Jesus said, "In the world you shall have tribulation: but be of good cheer; I have overcome the world." (John 16:33b). We can't afford to allow our way to become clouded by the things of this world, we must have clear vision and that vision must have Jesus in sight at all times. He is the One who makes the way for us to keep going. So, if it is a cracked windshield, a blown out tire, layoff from your job, bills piling up, or seemingly unanswered prayers, what do you do? You just can't see your way through, who do you go to, to straighten things out? Where do you go? Things are getting pretty cloudy and you can't see clearly. If you can't see where you are going, how can you lead someone else? Is God hearing you? "Lord, strengthen my faith!" Go to your pit stop; your team is standing right there; the Holy Ghost has everything you need!!! Listen to Him and do what He says. He is going to direct you back into the race.

Glimpses of Grace

Sometimes God allows us to be tested to see if we are going to drop out of the race or keep on going. There is no time to wallow around in self-pity. No racecar driver gets out of his car and stands around on the race track crying because he busted his tire or has a cracked windshield. Instead, he makes haste and gets to the pit stop. He knows where his help comes from. You don't have to be the first one to cross the finish line, but you do have to get there and cross it, and there is help along the way. "Wherefore seeing we also are compassed about with so great a cloud of witnesses, let us lay aside every weight, and the sin which doth so easily beset us, and let us run with patience the race that is set before us, Looking unto Jesus the author and finisher of our faith; Who for the joy that was set before Him endured the cross, despising the shame, and is set down at the right hand of the throne of God." (Heb. 12:1-2). Don't bypass your pit stop!!!

EMPTY VESSELS

In the Bible in the Book of Second Kings, there is a story of a widow woman with two sons, and she owed money that she could not pay. She called on Elisha to help her because the creditor was going to take her sons to be his slaves in payment of the money she owed. Elisha asked her what she had in her house. She told him that all she had was a pot of oil. (See 2 Kings 4:2&3). There are times when God allows us to get to our lowest ebb so He can show us just how great He is. We often tend to forget that "little is much in the Master's hand." The widow woman thought she only had an insignificant little pot of oil. She did not realize the power she had in her home. She did not realize she had all the resources she needed right there in her house!

Oil represents the Holy Ghost, and Jesus said, "Ye shall have power after that the Holy Ghost is come upon you: and ye shall be witnesses unto Me both in Jerusalem, and in all Judea, and unto the uttermost part of the earth." (Acts 1:8). When we have the Holy Ghost on the inside, the "pot of oil in our house," God will use us to fill a lot of empty vessels, if we let Him. He will enlarge our boarders so we can reach many souls for His kingdom, and they will also be full of the Holy Ghost and be able to be used by God. As long as there are vessels to fill, the oil doesn't run out. But we must be willing to listen and be obedient to the Master's voice. The widow woman didn't question Elisha at all. She didn't try to figure out what He was up to, nor did she feel, "He couldn't mean for me to do what he is telling me to do." She just stepped out on faith and followed Elisha's instructions. He told her to get empty vessels and make sure there was nothing in them, because he couldn't use them if they were not empty. God wants us to come before Him as empty vessels; no pride, no haughtiness, no feeling like "I can do this on my own, I don't need God's help," or, "I've been to school, I have a degree, I know what I am doing." Empty vessels! God can use empty vessels, and when He pours His Holy Spirit into empty vessels, they become powerhouses, and a powerhouse sends out electrical energy to other houses and "not a few," but to as many as you are willing to witness to.

What do you have in your house? If you have a little oil in your pot, God can take it and use it for His glory. Elisha told the widow woman to go to all her neighbors, not just those close by but go abroad and get empty vessels. There are empty vessels in our lives just waiting to be filled. Are we bringing them in? Are we using what we have in our houses, and being the witnesses for Christ He sent us out to be to our neighbors, far and wide? Step out on faith and use what you have; use what you have and watch God use what He has for you. "For we have this treasure in earthen vessels, that the excellency of the power may be of God, and not of us." (2 Cor. 4:7)

ENERGIZED BY THE PRESENCE OF GOD

When is the last time you felt the presence of God in your life in a way you could not describe? Maybe when you were in prayer, or ministering to someone, or worshiping God? There may have been times when all of a sudden you just began to cry and couldn't explain why. This is how it happens to me. I don't hear anything but I just feel His presence and I feel so loved by God. What a wonderful feeling!!! Are you in the position, spiritually, where God will speak to you in a very special way, to encourage you and energize you? Imagine how the disciples must have felt when Jesus came to them and told them to go and teach all nations. All nations? Without airplanes, trains, buses, or cars? This seemed like an impossible task, and I'm sure they had many questions. Then Jesus said, "and, lo, I Am with you alway, even unto the end of the world." (Matt. 28:20b). What a relief that must have been! The presence of Jesus always in their lives. We need to understand that God is everywhere, but not everywhere in the same way. He is everywhere present in our lives, but Proverbs 15:29 says, "The LORD is far from the wicked: but He heareth the prayers of the righteous." In the life of those who are sinful and far from Him, He is present in their lives in a very different way. We know He is present because He reigns on the just and the unjust.

Sometimes in our lives, God just "shows up." We are aware that He is doing something powerful in our life; we see Him moving and we know that it is nobody but God. He wants us to know Him personally in a real and living way, so that unmistakably we know that it is God Almighty. How do you define, "the presence of God?" The presence of God is God revealing Himself for a special purpose. This is why the place of the Holy Spirit in our lives is absolutely essential. When the Holy Spirit comes in, He regenerates us and gives us a new life, a life energized by His power, and it is this energizing power within us and overflowing which enables us to communicate with God. "They that worship God must worship Him in Spirit and in truth." (See John 4:24). God desires to make Himself known to us. He wants us to be able to feel His presence whenever He chooses to make Himself known, in an undeniable way. God makes Himself known in the way that will fit us individually. He appeared to Joshua in the form of an angel with a sword in His hand. The Lord visited Gideon and told him that he had too many men for God to give the Midianites into their hands. These men knew indeed that this was the presence of God, because they knew they would not have gone into battle the way God told them to go. He gave them clear directions on what to do and they followed those directions. Remember, He visited Moses in a burning bush. God's ways are awesome, and He has so many ways to manifest His glory in our lives.

Think about Peter in the presence of Jesus. He was able to walk on water; and as soon as he was out of the presence of Jesus, Peter denied Him three times. We have to stay close to Jesus and not walk "afar off" as Peter did. God has a plan, a purpose, and a will for our lives, and He is willing to get involved in our lives to fulfill what He desires for us. The presence of God is real! Pray and ask God to reveal Himself to you; tell Him that you are totally available to hear Him and to do His will and that you want Him to show up and reveal His presence in any way He wants to. We all have a tailor-made relationship with God. It fits you and no one else. He is a personal God. Think about this: there was only one incident of a burning bush; there was only one incident of a stone killing a giant; there was only one incident of a man walking on water; and there was only one incident of a man wrestling with an angel. When you are in the presence of God, you are able to see things from God's perspective. Remember the story of Elisha up against a mighty host, and his servant being fearful because there were so many. Elisha prayed and asked God to open the young man's eyes so he could see, and God showed the servant that the mountain was full of horses and chariots of fire surrounding Elisha. The presence of God truly energizes the believer so we have no need to fear anything. He enables us to see what no one else can see. Stay in the position where God can reveal

Himself to you whenever He wants to and how ever He wants to. "Thou wilt show me the path of life: in Thy presence is fullness of joy; at Thy right hand there are pleasures for evermore." (Ps. 16:11)

FIT FOR THE GARMENT

> "I will greatly rejoice in the LORD, my soul shall be joyful in my God; for He hath clothed me with the garments of salvation, He hath covered me with the robe of righteousness, as a bridegroom decketh himself with ornaments, and as a bride adorneth herself with her jewels." (Isa. 61:10)

Have you ever bought something to wear without trying it on and realized that it didn't fit right? It may be that you weren't the size you thought you were, but you wanted that garment so badly you decided to keep it and make yourself fit for the garment. That required much discipline in your eating habits, you would have to exercise vigorously, and you were determined to do whatever it took to be able to wear that beautiful garment. God our Father has a beautiful garment waiting to put on us, but we have to be fit in order to wear it. He has given us His robe of salvation and even His garment of praise, but He is still working on us so we will be able to wear His Robe of Righteousness. "And that ye put on the new man, which after God is created in righteousness and true holiness."

(Eph. 4:24). "Put on..", that indicates there is something *we* must do. The Bible tells us that once we are saved, have repented of our sins, and received Jesus in our hearts by faith, we are "new creatures in Christ Jesus." Paul is saying here, "act like it." Manifest in your daily life that you have a new relationship with the Father, and that you have been restored back to Him.

Well, how do we do that? Exercise, workout your salvation with "fear and trembling" (See Phil. 2:12-13), respecting and honoring God our Father, and being obedient to His will at all times. Just as a fitness instructor gives the exercises that will help us get in good physical condition and be able to fit the garment, so has Paul given in Colossians 3:1-17. In this chapter, he names the things we must take off and the things we must put on. We must first keep our mind on the things of the Kingdom of God, develop good habits, reading and studying the Word of God. Get rid of and destroy those things in our lives that will keep us from being fit for God's Robe of Righteousness. Remember, the old man is dead, and we must not allow him and his old ways to be resurrected in our lives. It will take an everyday, vigorous workout, but we can do all things through Christ who strengthens us. (See Phil. 4:13). Determine that you will be fit for the garment. "And to her was granted that she should be arrayed in fine linen, clean and white: for the fine linen is the righteousness of saints." (Rev. 19:8)

GOD CAN AND GOD WILL

> "And ye shall seek Me, and find Me, when ye shall search for Me with all your heart." (Jer. 29:13)

Many people pride themselves on being able to give great speeches and sound important. God is not impressed by our eloquent speech and big words, so that we are able to draw a crowd. Those things do not move Him. Paul said, "I came not with excellency of speech or of wisdom, declaring unto you the testimony of God." (I Cor. 2:1). God is moved by the heart that feels the burdens of this world and brings them to the altar. When we see the news and can pray and intercede for those in need, that is what moves Him. A selfless heart, a heart that is turned toward Him, a heart that seeks Him completely. He wants us to give our whole heart to Him, trusting Him without a shadow of doubt. God wants us to turn everything totally over to Him; He said according to your faith be it unto you. God wants to bless us more than we can imagine. He said we shall receive, if we ask trusting and believing that He will do what we ask. Seeking Him with the whole heart, nothing wavering, that is what moves the heart of God. We have to be expectant, knowing that He will. Our confidence in prayer is not based on our ability to speak, it is based on His ability to hear and understand what we are asking. He has great plans for us and we must expect Him to do great things for us. We limit God, forgetting that there is nothing He cannot do. God is the solution to our every problem; He has no problems. We can cast our burdens on Him and know that He knows just what to do with them. He will not leave us alone. He wants us to give our total lives to Him; our children, our finances, our marriage, our jobs, every sickness, and whatever we are carrying as a heavy burden. We cannot carry these loads. Jesus said, "Take My yoke upon you and learn from Me, for my yoke is easy and My burden is light." (See Matt. 11:28-30). Why should we even want to try to work it out on our own, knowing that we have a God who never fails? He is our Mighty Fortress, a Way Maker, our Healer, our Peace; let Him be who He is in your life. Acknowledge Him in all your ways and let Him direct your path. Follow His lead He gives us each day to give it back to Him. He is more than able to undertake and intervene on our behalf. God is a very present help in time of trouble. He is right here with us and will be with us every step of the way, if we trust Him. He wants to give us His peace in every situation. Think about who He says He is: He is our Shepherd, the Bread of Life, the Fount of Living Water, The Bright and Morning Star, our Light in the darkness, the Lifter up of our head, the Way the Truth and the Life, and more. Who wouldn't want to serve and trust a God like that?

Glimpses of Grace

Who is He in your life? Is He everything you need? Most of all, is He first in your life? When we put Him first, we will have no problem giving it all to Jesus, everything in our lives, knowing that God can, and God will. "Behold, I Am the LORD, the God of all flesh: is there anything too hard for Me?" (Jer. 32:27)

GOD HAS SAID, AND WE SAY

During the creation, God spoke words out of His mouth and everything He spoke came into existence, it all became something out of nothing. When you take time to really think about it, it really blows your mind! Something out of nothing by just speaking words, what a mighty God we serve.

Now, with that in mind, think of all the wonderful things God has spoken about us, His children. He has already spoken it out of His mouth, which means it is so, it does exist in our lives. All we have to do is grab hold to it by faith, believe that God's word is true (He is not a man that He should lie), and it is ours. How about this truth, "The LORD will make you the head, and not the tail. If you pay attention to the commands of the LORD your God that I give you this day and carefully follow them, you will always be at the top, never at the bottom." (Deut. 28:13). What position are you in at this moment? Are you under your circumstances? If so, why? God has already placed you at the top, and now you can say what God has said. His word has the same power today that it had when He first spoke it.

The word of God says, "Delight thyself also in the LORD; and He shall give thee the desires of thine heart. Commit thy way unto the LORD; trust also in Him; and He shall bring it to pass." (Ps. 37:4-5). Remember, God's word is His will, and it will not return back to Him without fulfilling what He wants it to do in our lives. "So shall My word be that goeth forth out of My mouth: it shall not return unto Me void, but it shall accomplish that which I please, and it shall prosper in the thing whereto I sent it." (Isa. 55:11). That means, when our desires are pleasing to the will of God, lining up with His word, He gives them to us. But the stipulation for the fulfillment of what God has spoken is written in Deuteronomy 28:13, as you read above, and also in Matthew 9:29, as Jesus healed the blind men, "Then He touched their eyes and said, "According to your faith let it be done to you." Those blind men trusted they were going to be able to see after Jesus touched them. That's it, obey God's word and by faith trust what He has said, and it shall be. There is an old hymn of the church that says, *"Trust and obey, for there is no other way to be happy in Jesus, but to trust and obey."*

God is true to His word, and we can know that His word is true. Just say what He has said. God's word says, "He giveth power to the faint; and to them that have no might He increaseth strength. But they that wait upon the LORD shall renew their strength; they shall mount up with wings as eagles; they shall run, and not be weary; and they shall walk, and not faint." (Isa. 40:29; 31). And now you can say, "I can do all things through Christ which strengtheneth me." (Phil. 4:13). The word of God says, "I have been young, and now am old; yet have I not seen the righteous forsaken, nor his seed begging bread." (Ps. 37:25). Therefore, you can now say, "But my God shall supply all your need according to His riches in glory by Christ Jesus." (Phil. 4:19). "Be careful for nothing; but in every thing by prayer and supplication with thanksgiving let your requests be made known unto God." (Phil. 4:6). Obey His word, believe that He will do what He has said, then you say what He has said, and by faith, see it done.

GOD'S WAYS ARE NOT OUR WAYS

God is an awesome God, and the Bible says that His ways are impossible for us to figure out. Our minds are too finite to be able to figure out the God who made the Universe, but sometimes we try to do it anyway. When we pray and expect Him to answer, we have it all planned what we want Him to answer; and we have the nerve to get upset if it doesn't come out the way we planned. But God is omniscient, He knows everything, and He knows what is best for us. He answers our prayers in the way He knows is best for us. You may have been praying for a certain job and didn't get it, but later you found the company shut down. God already knew, and He always has something better in mind.

Have you ever followed your GPS and it suddenly wanted to take you in another direction, and you began to complain and fuss wondering why it changed direction? So, you don't follow the GPS, you continue going in the same direction, then you get down the highway and find that there is a backup in traffic because of an accident and wish you had gone the way the GPS was telling you to go. We do that with God, don't we? We say, *"God can't be telling me to go this way, or do it this way, or say it this way, because that is not what I had planned."* The Word of God says that we make plans but God is the One who carries them out. We must learn to trust Him in everything, not just some things that seem easy, but in the hard things where there are disappointments and we can see no way it will work out for us. The Lord our God tells us that His ways are not our ways, He doesn't think the way we think. "For My thoughts are not your thoughts, neither are your ways My ways, saith the LORD. For as the heavens are higher than the earth, so are My ways higher than your ways, and My thoughts than your thoughts." (Isa. 55:8-9)

God knew us before we were born into this world. He has special plans for each of us and He knows what He has to do to carry out those plans, and He is going to do it His way. We make choices in life, some good and some bad, some right and some wrong. God always gives us chances to get it right and to follow His will for us. How do we know His will? I'm glad you asked. God's will is His Word. Read it, study it, meditate on it, and apply it to your life, and you won't go wrong. There is an old hymn of the church which sums it up so plainly:

> *"God moves in a mysterious way His wonders to perform; He plants His footsteps in the sea*
>
> *And rides upon the storm.*

Deep in unsearchable mines Of never failing skill He treasures up His bright designs And works His sovereign will.

Ye fearful saints, fresh courage take; The clouds you so much dread Are big with mercy and shall break In blessings on your head.

Judge not the Lord by feeble sense, But trust Him for His grace; Behind a frowning providence, He hides a smiling face.

His purposes will ripen fast, Unfolding every hour; The bud may have a bitter taste, But sweet will be the flower.

Blind unbelief is sure to err And scan His work in vain; God is His own interpreter, And He will make it plain." William Cowper, 1773.

"And we know that all things work together for good to them that love God, to them who are the called according to His purpose." (Rom. 8:28)

GROW WHERE YOU ARE PLANTED

"Now ye are the body of Christ and members in particular. And God hath set some in the church, first apostles, secondarily prophets, thirdly teachers, after that miracles, then gifts of healings, helps, governments, diversities of tongues." (1 Cor. 12:27-28)

The Lord was still showing me things about this repotted plant. Now that it had room to grow it was growing in leaps and bounds. New leaves began popping out all over the plant. Then, the Lord showed me where the new leaves were growing. They were growing in exactly the same place where the old leaves had dropped off. Every notch where there had been an old leaf, there was growing a new leaf. When God replants us in a larger place, He gets rid of everything that looked alright on the outside but was camouflaging the deadness on the inside. Those large leaves with yellowing edges eventually turned completely yellow and dropped off the plant, and many of them I pinched off because the roots where still trying to feed those dead leaves. God has to pinch off those things

Glimpses of Grace

that we still try to hold on to: past hurts, failures, disappointments, fears, and even relationships that are sucking the life out of our spiritual being and keeping us from growing where we are planted. Sometimes it's a painful struggle to make the change, and we find we cannot do it alone because it's too big for us to handle by ourselves. We cannot make the change in our life without the help of the Holy Spirit. Thanks be to God, that the Holy Spirit is ever present to help us. Our Lord Jesus Christ tells Him what to do, and He (the Holy Spirit) guides and directs us so we can become that member of the body of Christ we were predestinated to be; a prophet or teacher, worker of miracles, in the ministry of helps, or an apostle, etc.

I noticed that not one leaf on the plant was trying to jump in another leaf's place. They all had their own space to grow. There was no arguing, no jealousy, no envying, just perfect harmony. And as they all grew together the plant was becoming a beautiful sight to behold. When we as members of the body of Christ grow where we are planted, we become a joy to our Father and a beautiful sight for the world to see. "Only let your conversation be as it becometh the gospel of Christ; that whether I come and see you, or else be absent, I may hear of your affairs, that ye stand fast in one spirit, with one mind striving together for the faith of the gospel;" (Phil. 1:27)

INDESCRIBABLY DELICIOUS

Have you ever tasted something that was so good you just wanted to share it with someone else. Perhaps it was at a restaurant or maybe something you cooked yourself. You tasted it and said, "Wow! This is so good, (so and so) has got to taste this!" You just didn't want to keep that goodness to yourself and not share it, but you had to first taste it yourself before you could even try to tell someone how good it was. So many times we won't even try to taste something that is new to us, or we think it won't taste good. But how will you know whether you will like it or not if you don't taste it for yourself.

It's hard to imagine that a person can be ***indescribably delicious***, but that is exactly what Jesus is. The Word of God says, "O taste and see that the LORD is good: blessed is the man that trusteth in Him." (Ps. 34:80. Jesus said, "I Am the Bread of Life. I Am the living Bread which came down from heaven: if any man eat of this Bread he shall live forever: and the Bread that I will give is My flesh, which I will give for the life of the world." (John 6:48; 51). Now you know, that must be some really good tasting Bread!!! Remember the woman at the well, when Jesus asked her to give Him water to drink? Then He told her, "…but whoever drinks of the water that I will give him shall never thirst; but the water that I will give him will become in him a well of water springing up to eternal life." (John 4:4-26)

So, how do we taste Jesus? How do we eat and drink Him? Jesus is the Word made flesh, and when we feast on the Word, reading and studying the Bible, and applying it to our life, we are tasting of Jesus. This is the way we really get to know who He is, and we will find that He is extraordinary, unexplainable, miraculous, and very, very good! He has all the right ingredients instilled in Him and when we partake of Him those ingredients become a part of us, just as our natural food becomes a part of us. "But the fruit of the Spirit is love, joy, peace, long-suffering, gentleness, goodness, faith, Meekness, temperance:" (Gal. 5:22-23)

If you haven't already, may I encourage you to, *"taste and see that the LORD is good,"* and then share Him with someone else. You will find Him to be indescribably delicious!!!

IT IS ALWAYS TOO SOON TO QUIT

Have you ever wanted to quit everything in this life? Quit your family and all relationships, quit your job, even quit being spiritual and serving the Lord, quit being who you are? Then, you had a talk with God Almighty, your loving Father, and you discovered there really was no reason to want to quit. Our God is so understanding, He knows exactly how we feel and how we can become discouraged, so He gives the parable of the Fern and the Bamboo Tree.

God tells how He planted the fern and the bamboo tree seeds at the same time. He explained how He took very good care of them. He gave them light and water. Now, the fern grew quickly from the earth, and in no time its beautiful bright green leaves covered the ground. However, nothing came up from the bamboo seed. But God did not give up on it. In the second year, the fern grew even more vibrant, and spread its leaves abundantly. But still nothing from the bamboo seed. And even so, God did not give up or quit on the bamboo. In the third year, there was still nothing from the bamboo seed, but God did not quit or give up, He was persistent even up to the fifth year. Then it happened, a tiny sprout emerged from the earth. Now, compared to the fern which had been growing all these years, it was seemingly small and very insignificant, but that was just the beginning! For within six months that bamboo rose to over 100 feet tall. It had spent those five years growing roots, deep down in the earth. Those roots made it strong and gave it what it needed to survive. God says He will never put more on us than we can bear. (See I Cor. 10:13). When we are going through the trials and temptations, and all the struggles, we are actually growing roots. Just as God did not give up or quit on the bamboo, He will never give up or quit on us. We don't have to compare ourselves with others. God has a plan and a purpose for each of us that is different from any other of His creation. The fern has a different purpose than the bamboo, and they both have their own unique beauty.

Did you know that when the hurricane winds blow against the bamboo, it may bend as low as the ground, but it will not break because its roots are so deep? It comes right back to its very tall upright position, undaunted by the storm. "Let your roots grow down into Him, and your lives be built on Him. Then your faith will grow strong in the truth you were taught, and you will overflow with thankfulness." (Col. 2:7 NLT)

Everyone has days when they want to quit. When there are storms in life, struggles, intimidations, fears, all kinds of obstacles, just remember you are growing roots! Have a talk with the Father and find out what His purpose is for you. Always remember, He said He would never leave you nor forsake you. He will be with you until the end of the world. (See Heb. 13:5b). Don't quit, don't give up on God! "Therefore, my beloved brethren, be ye steadfast, unmovable, always abounding in the work of the Lord, forasmuch as ye know that your labour is not in vain in the Lord." (1 Cor. 15:58)

PATIENCE IS A VIRTUE

We are called the "Microwave Generation," and rightly so. We want everything done in a hurry, and now, even the microwave isn't fast enough. We are so impatient when we find we have to wait. We even try to hurry God, not realizing He has His own timetable, His own schedule, and it can't be rushed. Sometimes we have to accept the fact that He may put us on "Hold," and when He does we must watch what we say and be careful what we speak out of our mouths. Just as that small rudder on a big ship can move the ship in different directions, our tongues, though they may be small, can move things, situations, and circumstances in either negative or positive directions. We must not allow the enemy of our souls to fill our minds with all kinds of negative things so we don't trust God and His Word. Our mind is a garden and the seeds we plant and allow others to plant in our minds are what we will reap. If we are constantly thinking negative thoughts because things are not working out the way we expect them to, or as fast as we think they should, then we shouldn't expect more than what we believe. Jesus said, "According to your faith, be it unto you." (See Matt. 9:29). What we think is what we speak out of our mouths, and that's what we put into the atmosphere, because our words are life, they are alive and will produce what we say. When we are going through trials and tribulations in our lives, problems in our home with children, spouses, problems on the job, money running out before the month, whatever the case may be, we cannot, I repeat, **we cannot** allow our emotions to get the best of us. We cannot allow our mouths to speak according to what we see. ***Our expectation is from God***, and He is working all the time on our behalf, for our good and for His glory. He always has a plan and a purpose for everything He does in our lives and everything He allows to happen in our lives. ***What is He teaching you*** while you are on "hold?" How about love and forgiveness? Is there some relationship you need to get right? Well, guess what?! God is patiently waiting for you to do your part, then He will do His part. We have to be in the place of blessing in order to receive the blessings from God. As we wait patiently, without complaining, only trusting that God is faithful and always keeps His promises, we will begin to see the manifestation of our breakthrough. Praise Him in the "waiting room," He lives in our praises! And always be, "Rejoicing in hope; patient in tribulation; continuing instant in prayer." (Rom. 12:12)

POSITION YOURSELF FOR TRANSFORMATION

There was a famine in Bethlehem (the House of Bread), so Naomi and her family moved to Moab. Now, Naomi is a widow and both her sons have died. Their wives are left with Naomi and she encouraged them to go home to their family. Ruth wants to stay with Naomi and she is determined to do so. But Ruth replied, "Don't ask me to leave you and turn back. I will go wherever you go and live where you live. Your people will be my people, and your God will be my God. I will die where you die and will be buried there. May the LORD punish me severely if I allow anything but death to separate us." (Ruth 1:16-17 NLT). Apparently, Ruth is influenced by the life Naomi lives and she wants to follow her. We never know how people are watching us and are being blessed because they see the love of God in us. When we live our life according to the will of God, others are blessed. Ruth positioned herself for transformation. She meets Boaz, a rich relative of Naomi's deceased husband, when they return to Bethlehem, and finds favor in his sight. He allows her to glean in his field as much as she wants to and as much as she needs to, and now Naomi is being blessed by Ruth. When Naomi discovered that Ruth was gleaning in Boaz's field she had a plan that would position Ruth for transformation. Ruth was humble and willing to do exactly as Naomi instructed. When we walk in the humility of Jesus, God will bless us abundantly.

Naomi told Ruth to wait until Boaz was asleep and then to uncover his feet and lay at his feet. When he awakened and discovered Ruth at his feet, she asked him to cover her with his skirt. Boaz was pleased that Ruth had chosen him to be her cover. Placing his skirt over her indicated that he agreed to take responsibility for her; he was agreeing to marry her. Ruth was positioning herself for transformation. Before the foundation of the world, God had this plan for Ruth. She had no idea that she would set in motion a chain of events that would blow her mind. First, she married a wealthy farmer in Bethlehem. Second, she became the mother of Obed, the father of Jesse; and Jesse was the father of David, who became king of Israel, and ancestor to the King of kings, Jesus the Savior of the world. Ruth positioned herself in Moab for transformation by marrying Naomi's son. She went from rags to riches. She went from being a gentile outcast to being an ancestor of Jesus, Emmanuel.

We can position ourselves for transformation and watch God work miracles in our lives. Watch your latter days be the best days of your life. You will receive blessings you can't imagine. Ruth's life began to change when she decided to serve Jehovah God. It starts when you put Christ first in your life. "But seek ye first, the kingdom of

God, and His righteousness; and all these things shall be added unto you." (Matt. 6:33) "Not my will, but Thy will be done." (Luke 22:42b). "Present your bodies a living sacrifice, holy, and acceptable unto God, which is your reasonable service. And be not conformed to this world: but be ye transformed by the renewing of your mind, that ye may prove what is that good, and acceptable, and perfect, will of God." (Rom. 12:1-2)

IT IS WELL WITH MY SOUL

"Can anything ever separate us from Christ's love? Does it mean He no longer loves us if we have trouble or calamity, or are persecuted, or are hungry or cold or in danger or threatened with death? (Even the Scriptures say, "For Your sake we are killed every day, we are being slaughtered like sheep.") No, despite all these things, overwhelming victory is ours through Christ, Who loved us. And I am convinced that nothing can ever separate us from His love. Death can't, and life can't. The angels can't, and the demons can't. Our fears for today, our worries about tomorrow, and even the powers of hell can't keep God's love away. Whether we are high above the sky or in the deepest ocean, nothing in all creation will ever be able to separate us from the love of God that is revealed in Christ Jesus our Lord." Romans 8:35-39 (NLT).

The song, *"It Is Well With My Soul,"* (Horatio G. Spafford), sings often in my spirit. The Lord has been showing me that no matter what is going on in our life, we can say, "It is well with my soul." It is easy to say it when everything is going well in our life. No stress, no strain, no sickness, no pain, no loss, and only gain; oh yes, it is easy then to say, "It is well with my soul." But what about when things are not going so well? What about in times

Glimpses of Grace

of sorrow and sadness, or times when we can't seem to make ends meet before the money runs out? What about when the devil is running rampant in our family? Or the times when we are having so much pain in our body we can't seem to function right? Can we still say, "It is well with my soul?" Of course, we can! When we are going through these trials and tribulations, which are inevitable as long as we are in this life, we have the blessed assurance of knowing that none of these things shall move us from our position of salvation through Jesus Christ our Lord. And that is the most important fact of the matter.

Let's face it, the devil hates us and each one of us is *number on*e on his *hit list*. He is going to try to do all that he can to steal, kill, and destroy everything in our life that looks like Jesus. That is his job and he does it well, because he hates Jesus most of all. But Romans the 8th Chapter tells us that we are **more** than conquerors through Him that loved us. As long as we have our faith and trust in Jesus it doesn't matter about the circumstances around us because our circumstances do not have control over the position of our soul and our relationship with God the Father. When we think about what Jesus has done for us on Calvary, we can certainly say, "It is well with my soul." Romans 8:39 says that **nothing** can separate us from the love of God, which is in Christ Jesus our Lord. When we have this confidence settled down in our innermost being, we can know without a shadow of a doubt that our soul is anchored in Jesus and we shall not be moved.

It is written in Habakkuk 3:17-19, "Even though the fig trees have no blossoms, and there are no grapes on the vine; even though the olive crop fails, and the fields lie empty and barren; even though the flocks die in the fields, and the cattle barns are empty, yet I will rejoice in the LORD! I will be joyful in the God of my salvation. The Sovereign LORD is my strength! He will make me as surefooted as a deer and bring me safely over the mountains." Now that is truly trusting in the Lord and being able to say, "It is well with my soul," because trusting in Jesus gives us that inner peace and joy. The last verse of the song goes like this, *"And, Lord haste the day when the faith shall be sight, The clouds be rolled back as a scroll, The trump shall resound and the Lord shall descend, Even so, it is well with my soul!"* And nothing in this life shall be able to keep us from that appointment with our Lord and Savior Jesus Christ! "Rejoice in the LORD always: and again I say Rejoice." (Phil. 4:4)

THE MORE WE GIVE THE MORE WE HAVE

In the Book of Acts, while Paul was in Miletus on his way to Jerusalem, he sent for the elders of the church in Ephesus. When they came to him, he gave his last instructions on how to take care of the congregation, feeding them with the Word of God, and warning them to watch, for the enemy was going to come in and try to draw disciples for themselves. He reminded them that Jesus said, "It is more blessed to give than to receive." (Acts 20:35). Why did Jesus say that? He wanted us to know that the more we give of ourselves, our talents, our tithes, and our offerings, the more we will receive. We can never give more than what the Father will give back to us. Love motivates us to give with a willing heart. Jesus loved us so much that He was willing to lay down His life for us. He gave us His all, holding back nothing. "Who for the joy that was set before Him endued the cross, despising the shame, and is set down at the right hand of the throne of God." (Heb. 12:2b). Jesus gave His all and in the end He had more than He had before; He had souls to present to the Father, those who would be with Him throughout eternity.

When we open our hearts and hands to give to God, He takes what we give and multiplies it according to His calculations and uses it for His glory. Then, He fills our hearts and hands according to His riches in glory, with His abundant blessings. Jesus said, "Give, and it shall be given unto you; good measure, pressed down, and shaken together, and running over, shall men give into your bosom. For with the same measure that ye mete withal it shall be measured to you again." (Luke 6:38). Whatever we give to others, that is what we will receive back. If we give out of the abundance of our hearts, with willingness and love, the Father will multiply it back to us, a thousand times over. If we give stingily and hold back, don't expect to receive an abundant blessing. It's not all about money, which is the first thing that pops into the mind when you say "give." There is so much more God wants us to give that we are not willing to give. He wants our whole heart, first of all, and once He has that, the rest of the giving is easy. "I beseech you therefore, brethren, by the mercies of God, that ye present your bodies a living sacrifice, holy, acceptable unto God, which is your reasonable service." (Rom. 12:1)

God has given each of us gifts and talents to be used for His glory and kingdom and to be a blessing to those whom He places in our lives. How many blessings have we held back from someone, and how many blessings have we not received from the Father? Jesus said, "Inasmuch as you have done it unto one of the least of these My brethren, you have done it unto Me." (Matt. 25:35-40). You see, when we give abundantly, the blessings come back to us from God, and He never runs out. "Every man according as he purposeth in his heart, so let him give; not grudgingly, or of necessity: for God loveth a cheerful giver. And God is able to make all grace abound toward you; that ye, always having all sufficiency in all things, may abound to every good work." (2 Cor. 9:7-8). The Father loves those who give with a glad heart. He would rather us give one penny with love than thousands with bitterness and hatred in our hearts. "Now unto Him that is able to do exceeding abundantly above all that we ask or think, according to the power that worketh in us." (Eph. 3:20). God always gives back abundantly.

PREPARATIONS FOR MOVING

I remember when my husband and I decided to sell our home after thirty-seven years and move with our daughter and her family. There was a lot of preparation that had to be done. An inspector had to come to see if the house was in good order to be sold, and if not, he told us what we had to have done to make it the way he felt it should be. As far as we could see, it was a good house and in good condition with many upgrades inside and outside. But low and behold, the inspector found some things that needed to be changed! Even though the roof was not leaking, he wanted tar on the roof. We had to have a slope in the kitchen floor jacked up; a slope which had been there since the original owner had the basement entrance changed from the kitchen to the dining room, and it was quite unnoticeable.

In Colossians the third chapter, verses 1-9, 13, & 14, Paul is writing to the church in Colossae admonishing them to get their "house" in order in preparation for their moving day. He was letting them know that this was not their final home; that there was going to be a moving day and the Holy Ghost, who is the Inspector, is checking some things that need to be changed. Their roof needed some reinforcement, so they were told to keep their minds stayed on Jesus; think on things above, spiritual things and don't get caught up in the things of this world. Disobedience can make an awful slope in your life, so jack it up with the obedience of the Lord Jesus Christ. He was obedient even unto death. Those changes and repairs the inspector told us to have done cost us money, and I really squawked about having to do them because I didn't feel it was necessary to do everything he wanted done. Getting our spiritual house in order is going to cost us and we don't always want to pay the price, but the Holy Ghost says it is necessary for our moving preparation.

I had no idea we had accumulated so much stuff that we couldn't take with us. My husband was in the hospital by this time so I couldn't depend on him to help me. We will find that as we prepare to move out of this life to our final destination, there will be people who we thought we could depend on, but who will be totally unavailable. "Set your affection on things above, not on things on the earth." (Col. 3:2). Even though we know we will be moving, we don't know when the settlement date will be. We just have to be ready. I knew our settlement date and it took a while before I could start packing up. I had so much stuff to get rid of, and I didn't know where to start. There was furniture, dishes, clothing, and a lot of "trash" in the basement. I had to make sure I separated the good stuff from the trash. God says, "Be ye holy for I Am holy." (1 Pet. 1:16). If there is anything in our life that doesn't represent the holiness of God, we must get rid of it. There may even be some good things, but if it is cluttering our life and keeping us too busy to do what God wants us to do, get rid of it.

Moving preparation is hard work but we must stick with it until it is finished. Jesus said he that endures until the end shall be saved. Allow the Holy Spirit to inspect your house and do whatever He says you need to do in preparation for your moving day. "In My Father's house are many mansions: if it were not so, I would have told you. I go to prepare a place for you. And if I go and prepare a place for you, I will come again, and receive you unto Myself; that where I Am, there ye may be also." (John 14:2-3)

KEEP YOUR BAG PACKED

Some people do a lot of traveling and are constantly packing their luggage. My mother had a friend who never emptied her luggage because she traveled a lot. Well, it depends on where you are going, what you carry in your bag. One year, my sister and I traveled together to our family reunion in Myrtle Beach, South Carolina. Now, my sister is a real bag packer. She will start packing weeks ahead of her trip, putting things in her bag as she remembers them, and making sure she doesn't forget anything. I, on the other hand, am a last-minute packer, especially my clothes because I can't stand how they get wrinkled in the suitcase. So of course, at the last minute I am running around trying to make sure I didn't leave out anything. How many of you know that it is best to pack your things as you think about them, instead of waiting until the last minute?

First of all, we had to realize that we were flying and there are many rules, regulations, and instructions we have to take into consideration, including your arrival time at the airport (at least two hours before your flight). Your bags have to be a certain weight and size, and the number of bags you can carry on the airplane. We all need to pack our bags with our mind on that flight we have

Glimpses of Grace

to take. Jesus said He is coming back for those who are looking for His appearing. We've got to have our bags and tickets ready. There are some things we dare not try to place in our bags because there is a scanner at the safety check that will reveal what is in your bag. The Holy Ghost is our "Scanner," and He will reveal what is in our bags. In God's Word, it tells us what we can't take with us. (See Col. 3:5-9). We must get rid of all earthy sinful things lurking within us: sexual sins, lust, impurity, and shameful desires. You cannot pack this stuff in your travel bag. You can't be greedy and full of idolatry. Don't pack anger, rage, and malicious behavior in your bag, or talking evil about people and using dirty language. Remember, what comes out of the mouth is coming from the heart. Life and death are in the power of the tongue, and when you curse someone you are dealing death to that soul. We cannot pack this garbage in our bags because the "Scanner" will pick it up, and the "Security Guard," which is the Word of God, will tell you that you have to get rid of it if you want to get on that flight. You will have to get rid of lying of any kind; living it, speaking it, and acting it; none of it will pass the "Scanner."

Now these are the clothes you may take with you. In fact, you are required to take these items on this flight: tenderhearted mercy and kindness, because someone is going to need you to help them along the way. They may need you to direct them to a certain place in the airport of life. You will also need humility, because someone will inevitably get in your way and try to make you stumble with their baggage, so they can be first in line to get on the flight. If we all have our ticket, it doesn't matter who gets on first, your seat is already reserved. You will need to pack gentleness and patience, because sometimes there may seem to be a delay in the time of the arrival of your flight, and because we don't know what is happening, we tend to become impatient. But God is the Pilot in control, and He is working it out, and the flight will arrive and leave on time, according to God's time schedule. We must pack forgiveness, because sometimes along the trip you may feel a cool breeze of offense, and forgiveness will keep you warm and comfortable. Most of all, we must pack love. This is the most important piece of clothing in our bag. It goes with everything else we have to wear, and it compliments every other garment in our bag.

There are large wastebaskets in the scanning area so that as you go through, you can discard what you can't take with you. If you haven't already, start packing now! Pack carefully and keep your bag packed. "And whosoever you do in word or deed, do all in the Name of the Lord Jesus, giving thanks to God and the Father by Him." (Col. 3:17)

MAGNIFY THE LORD

> "I will bless the LORD at all times: His praise shall continually be in my mouth. My soul shall make her boast in the LORD: the humble shall hear thereof and be glad. O magnify the LORD with me; and let us exalt His Name together." (Ps. 34:1-3)

To magnify something means to make it bigger in our sight, we see it many times bigger than without the magnifying glass. The Word of God says to magnify the Lord. Whenever David was in trouble, he magnified the Lord, and then the praises would come forth. When he went before Goliath, He went *"in the Name of the Lord."* Even though Goliath was over nine feet tall, David saw God much bigger than that giant and he approached him *"in the Name of the Lord."* There is no other name under the heaven given among men that can save us; only Jesus. He saves us from sin and every other giant that would come against us when we magnify Him and see Him bigger in every situation. When Moses sent the twelve spies into the promised land for Israel, ten came back terribly afraid because the men were giants. They said, *"we are grasshoppers compared to them."* Don't you know that when

Glimpses of Grace

you see yourself as a grasshopper, your enemy will see you like that too? Only two of the spies remembered how God had delivered them many times before, and trusted that He would do the same in that situation. Elisha was surrounded by armies ready to take him out. The young servant with him was afraid of that great mass, but Elisha was not intimidated by what he could see with his natural eye. He prayed and asked God to open the young man's eyes so he would see with his spiritual eyes. "Then the LORD opened the servant's eyes, and he looked and saw the hills full of horses and chariots of fire all around Elisha." (2 Kings 6:17 NIV). Elisha magnified the Lord and saw there were more with him than those who were against him. God is always greater! We serve a great big, wonderful God!

You know how some children like to brag about their dad, and they boast about how big he is and what he can do better than anyone else's dad? They magnify him and that is how they see him. We have to stop putting our Daddy, "Abba, Father," in a box and see Him as great as He is. "For ye have not received the spirit of bondage again to fear; but ye have received the Spirit of adoption, whereby we cry, Abba, Father". (Rom. 8:15). He is the God of all flesh and there is nothing too hard for Him. Whether your giant is spiritual, physical, mental, or financial, our Daddy is rich in every way; He is the owner of the cattle on a thousand hills, and all the silver and gold belong to Him. He is rich in houses and land, and He holds the wealth of the world in His hand. "But my God shall supply all your need according to His riches in glory, by Christ Jesus." (Phil. 4:19). "Greater is He that is in you than he that is in the world." (1 John 4:4). Therefore, "I can do all things through Christ which strengtheneth me." (Phil. 4:13). Got any rivers you need to cross; He opened the Red Sea. Got any mountains you cannot climb or tunnel through, He made the mountains.

In every situation and circumstance in life, boast on our Daddy and magnify Him; the Great God Almighty, Creator of heaven and earth. There is no one Greater! He specialized in the things we think are impossible. "Thine O LORD, is the greatness, and the power, and the glory, and the victory, and the majesty: for all that is in the heaven and in the earth is Thine: Thine is the kingdom, O LORD, and Thou art exalted as head above all. Both riches and honour come of Thee, and Thou reignest over all; and in Thine hand is power and might; and in Thine hand it is to make great, and to give strength unto all." (1 Chron. 29:11-12)

MAKE EVERY DAY A MASTERPIECE

Are we truly thankful to God for every day that He gives us? Do we live every day as though it is our last day on earth? What if a doctor diagnosed you with some dreaded terminal disease and told you that you had a very limited time to live; how would you live your life from that time forward? Would you change what you usually do each day; would you change your attitude about some things? God gives us new mercies each day. He allows us to wake up and live a new day just to glorify Him. Jesus tells us not to worry about tomorrow, but let tomorrow take care of itself. We need to learn to live like we are dying. Paul says, "I die daily." We need to live each day with a constant dying to self. Don't take people and things for granted. When is the last time you told someone you love them? Your husband, your children, your sister, your brother? Do you go to work each day dreading your job, and just wishing for the day you can retire? God wants you to live for the moment, enjoying the moment you are in right now. In other words, be where you are, and live in the place where you are at this present time. Can you focus on what you are doing right now without thinking about where you should be one hour from now, or even five minutes from now? We rush through one part of our day to get to the next part. We rush through breakfast so we can plan for lunch time. We rush through lunch time so we can start preparing dinner. We rush through dinner so that we can relax before bedtime. We rush through one day to get to the next. We don't take time to see and hear what is around us because we are so busy rushing to the next thing. We sit in traffic complaining about not being able to rush through it. We need to take the time to see the people around us sitting in the traffic and take a moment to say a prayer for them. God has you in that place at that time as a part of His plan for you on that particular day. Psalm 37:23 says, "The steps of a good man are ordered by the LORD." He had you right there when that accident happened so that you could pray. Think about it, if you hadn't been a little slower than usual, you would have missed the opportunity. Accentuate the positive! See something good in everything. During the creation, over and over again, God said, "That's good." We need to see things through the eyes of God.

The time we have is but a fleeting moment. "For a thousand years in Thy sight are but as yesterday when it is past, and as a watch in the night." (Ps. 90:4). Verse 12 says, "So teach us to number our days, that we may apply our hearts unto wisdom". The next day, the next moment isn't promised to us. This is the only chance you have to live this day. Let the light of Jesus shine through you this day. Give someone their flowers today, while they can smell them. "And let the beauty of the LORD our God be upon us." (Ps. 90:17). Take the part of the day that God has given you, and live it to the fullest, for His glory. Smell the flowers, and listen to the birds sing. Make yourself totally available to Him, without your own agenda. Just give the day back to Him, along with yourself, so that His kingdom may come and His will be done, to the glory and praise of His holy Name. Make today a "Masterpiece," because it was truly made by the Master. "This is the day which the LORD hath made; we will rejoice and be glad in it." (Ps. 118:24)

RELEASE YOUR POTENTIAL

Those of you who have children, how many of you have gazed at that little gift from God and have spoken over their life, that which you see them to be in the future? And as they begin to grow, you cultivate the potential you see, leading them in the right direction to fulfill that destiny. Well, God has a potential in each one of us that He has placed in us to be used for His glory. There is so much in us that we haven't even tapped into the surface. We expose only the tip of the iceberg, but God knows what is on the inside, what He has placed there, and for some reason, or many reasons, we fail to let that potential be released in our life. We are destined for greatness; we are the children of God and He has great plans for us. "For I know the plans I have for you," declares the LORD, "plans to prosper you and not to harm you, plans to give you hope and a future." (Jer. 29:11 NIV)

Fear will hold you back and keep you from being all that God wants you to be. People in your life may have told you that you will never be able to accomplish your dream. They instilled doubt in your mind about yourself and who you are, what you can do, or cannot do. But when we stop listening to people and listen to what God has to say about

Glimpses of Grace

us, we will be able to release our potential and be all that we are meant to be in this life, to the glory of God. He has not given us the spirit of fear, but of power, of love, and of a sound mind. (See 2 Tim. 1:7). When we step out on faith, trusting that God is holding our hand, holding us up, we can stand on His Word that says, "I can do all things through Christ which strengthenth me." (Phil. 4:13)

Oh yes, you have the potential to scale that six-foot wall and slay any giant; you can shout until the walls come crumbling down. "No weapon that is formed against thee shall prosper; and every tongue that shall rise against thee in judgment thou shalt condemn. This is the heritage of the servants of the LORD, and their righteousness is of Me, saith the LORD." (Isa. 54:17). It's in you, it's in me. "The LORD is my light and my salvation; whom shall I fear? the LORD is the strength of my life; of whom shall I be afraid?" (Ps. 27:1). "What shall we then say to these things? If God be for us, who can be against us?" (Rom. 8:31)

Step out into the unknown, come out of your comfort zone. Get out of the ship and walk on the water. Use what is in your hand, stretch out your rod of faith, see the waters part, and walk over on dry ground. Remember, you are never walking alone. God is right there with you guiding every step of the way. You don't have to be afraid of failing because there is no failure in God. "I will instruct thee and teach thee in the way which thou shalt go: I will guide thee with Mine eye." (Ps. 32:8). Release your potential.

RESURRECTION POWER

We can read the Word of God, memorize it and have it in our head, knowing it backwards and forwards. But if we do not apply it to our life it really means nothing, and we cannot apply it to our lives if we do not have it in our heart. Jesus is the Word made flesh and He has to become flesh in us. After the Resurrection, Jesus said that all power in heaven and earth had been given to Him. There is no greater power on earth or in heaven, Jesus is All!

In order to have Resurrection Power we have to walk in HUMILITY. Jesus walked in humility throughout His earthly life. Humbleness is not an option; it is essential if we want to walk with God. Humility is not weakness, it is strength and power under control, with the Holy Ghost in control. "But ye shall receive power, after that the Holy Ghost is come upon you." (Acts 1:8). Backing down from a fight doesn't mean you are a "fraidy cat" and scared. Jesus taught to be a peacemaker. If we believe we are always right and can't admit that we fail and make mistakes, we are walking in pride. God promises to exalt the humble, not the proud. (See James 4:10). Identifying with Jesus, no matter what the reaction of others may be, demands a dying to self and giving up our own "rights." Actually, we lost our rights in the Garden of Eden. Paul says, "I die

Glimpses of Grace

daily." (See 1 Cor. 15:31). We have to beat down that "old man" that tries to rise up in us, because we have been risen to a new life in Christ Jesus. "He hath shewed thee, O man, what is good; and what doth the LORD require of thee, but to do justly, and to love mercy, and to walk humbly with thy God?" (Mic. 6:8). God resists the proud and gives grace to the humble. "Humble yourselves therefore under the mighty hand of God, that He may exalt you in due time:" (1 Pet. 5:6)

The Resurrection life of Jesus dictates that we walk in OBEDIENCE. Jesus took on Himself the form of a servant, and He said He came to serve. He was obedient unto the death on the cross. He never made Himself to be equal with God. (See Phil. 2:5-11). Whatever we have to go through in this life will never match what Jesus suffered for us, and remember, He did no wrong. He said as He was in this world so shall we be. We will have haters and enemies, but we must remain faithful to Jesus Christ, in spite of it all. When we are obedient to the Lord Jesus Christ, He gives us power over all the powers of the enemy. We can tear down the devil's strongholds and put him in his place. We can knock down every wall that is built up to keep men from finding Him. We have to do this first in ourselves, then we can reach others who walk in disobedience. We have to practice what we preach and teach!

The Resurrection life of Jesus shows itself in HOLINESS. Jesus now has the authority to give and share the life of God to and with us. Once the Holy Spirit comes in, our

Glimpses of Grace

whole life changes; we now live our lives in the light of Jesus' life. All comparisons are made according to God 's standard and not man's. The Holy Spirit does in us all that Jesus died to make us be. "It is not by might, nor by power, but by My Spirit, saith the LORD of hosts." (Zech. 4:6). We cannot make ourselves Holy but we can yield to the Holy Spirit and He gets the work done. It's an inside job which shows up on the outside. We have this "treasure in earthen vessels," and God knows our frailties. He is never going to tell us to do something we cannot do without enabling us by His power to do it. "And be found in Him, not having mine own righteousness, which is of the law, but that which is through the faith of Christ, the righteousness which is of God by Faith: That I may know Him, and the power of His resurrection, and the fellowship of His sufferings, being made conformable unto His death.;" (Phil. 3:9-10)

RISE UP AND WALK

When Peter and John were going into the temple to pray, there was a lame man who had been lame all his life. He reached out to Peter and John for them to give him money. Peter's response to the man was, "Look on us." The man did as he was instructed, expecting to receive money from Peter and John. But he received more than he expected. Peter told him that he had no money to give him, but what he had, he would give him that. Peter was filled with the power of the Holy Ghost, and the works that Jesus did he was able to do also. This is what Jesus meant when He said that we would do greater works than He did on the earth. When Peter said, "In the Name of Jesus Christ of Nazareth rise up and walk," that man did not hesitate to take Peter's hand and get up from the ground. (See Acts 3:1-16). And Peter, with holy boldness, did not doubt that Jesus would heal the lame man. What faith and confidence on the part of both Peter and the lame man! How many of us would have had that kind of faith and trust in God?

In order for the power of God to be made manifested in the lives of those we touch, we must first believe in our hearts that God will do what He says He will do. Jesus said if we believe and not doubt in our heart, that we could ask what we want and it will be given unto us. We have to rise up and walk the walk of faith before we can help someone else. The confidence is not in ourselves, but in the living God. Jesus said that whatever we ask in His Name, the Father will give it unto us. As believers in Christ Jesus, filled with the Holy Spirit, we have that same power within us that Peter and John had. Would you be willing to say to someone, "Rise up and walk," knowing they had been born lame? We think about what *we can do* and doubt that it will happen for us. Jesus is Jehovah Rapha, He is the Healer, but He is willing to use us if we make ourselves totally available to Him. We must rise up and walk in the faith of the Son of God who loved us and gave Himself for us. In Him we live and move and have our being. Absolutely, we can do nothing without Him, but thanks be to God who gives us the victory to be able to do all things through Christ who strengthens us.

God will not give His glory to another, and when the people ran to Peter and John because they saw the lame man walking, Peter said to them, "Why are you looking at us as though we by our own power or holiness made this man walk?" (Acts 3:12). He let them know that it was the man's faith in Jesus that healed him. Activate your faith, rise up and walk in the Name of Jesus, so that that lame person in your life may be able to grab hold to your hand and by faith, get up off the ground, and walk, too. "If you abide in Me, and My words abide in you, you shall ask what you will, and it shall be done unto you. Herein is My Father glorified, that you bear much fruit; so shall you be My disciples." (John 15:7-8)

THE ORDER OF THE TOWEL

> "Jesus, knowing that the Father had given all things into His hands, and that He had come from God and was going to God, rose from supper and laid aside His garments, took a towel and girded Himself. After that, He poured water into a basin and began to wash the disciples' feet, and to wipe them with the towel with which He was girded." (John 13:3-5)

It's hard for us to imagine Jesus, our Lord and Savior, bowing down and washing someone's feet. The disciples did not have time to wash their feet and make sure they were clean, as we do when we have foot-washing in our churches. We will wash our feet and put lotion on them before we will allow someone else to wash them. But Jesus washed those smelly, dusty, dirty feet. He took the position of a slave servant. The servant always washed the feet of the guests.

Think about those of us who want to be "up front." The world says we have made it when we move from the back to the front; when we move from the back table and the side table, to the head table. Here, Jesus left the head table and bowed down to wash dirty feet. He said if you want to be a blessing and be blessed, you must belong to the Order of the Tower. Be willing to pick up your towel and wash feet. We see Jesus with Judas, the one who was going to betray Him, and without hesitation Jesus washed his feet. We can't pick and choose whose feet we are going to wash. Jesus called each of us to be a servant. We have to be willing to yield ourselves to those who allow the devil to use them. They treat us mean and nasty for no reason, and Jesus says, "Wash their feet." They are in the work place, in our families, and among our friends. Jesus, by example, teaches us to take a towel and serve them. He wants us to serve those who are unlovely. Don't forget about Peter. Peter was going to deny Jesus three times within a few hours, saying that He never knew Jesus. Yet, Jesus willingly washed his feet. Peter was afraid when he should have been strong. We have those in our lives whom we can call "***fair weather friends.***" When things are going well they are praising the Lord and hanging around you all the time; you can't get rid of them. But as soon as a storm comes, they are off and running; they can't be found. We have couples getting married one day, and before the ink is dry on the paper, they are running in opposite directions. They can't stand the rough places, and as soon as the going gets tough, they get going. We have those people in our lives who said they would stick with us through "thick and thin," but when they are put to the test with trials and tribulations they can't be found.

Then, we have the other ten disciples who were selfish; they were concerned about themselves. They couldn't imagine Jesus washing their feet, but when the odds seemed to be against them they all left Him, just a short time later. They were looking out for number one, themselves. What would you have done? Would you be loyal and true in spite of tough times? It takes true humility and a servant's heart to be willing to put others first, thinking of their well-being, and to love them no matter what. That's what Jesus did. Do you have your towel?

HAVING THE MIND OF CHRIST

"Let this mind be in you, which was also in Christ Jesus: Who being in the form of a man, thought it not robbery to be equal with God: But made of Himself no reputation, and took upon Him the form of a servant, and was made in the likeness of men: And being found in fashion as a man, He humbled Himself, and became obedient unto death, even the death of the cross." (Phil. 2:5-8)

When Jesus washed His disciples' feet He was demonstrating true humility. If you can be a servant (a **humble** servant), working with people who get on your last nerve, being nice to those who are not nice, being kind to those who speak ill of you, and loving the unlovely, you are on your way for a blessing. Try it today, and see what happens. Jesus was able to do this because He lived by the plan of God. He did not operate by an agenda He had set for Himself. When He was twelve years old, Jesus asked His parents when they were frantically looking for Him, *"Know you not, that I must be about my Father's business?"*

Glimpses of Grace

Jesus indicated that He does nothing of Himself; He took His orders from God His Father. Whatever we do, make sure we don't do it without the leading of the Lord. If you can't do it in front of Jesus, don't do it! All that Jesus did was a part of God's plan. He was sure the Father had a plan for His life. Being a Christian is not easy, but it is part of the plan of God for each of us. The situation may be uncomfortable, but it is part of the plan. We can serve in the midst of the storm, among the unloving, the scared, and the selfish, when we know that God has a plan for our life. When we are sure about what God has for us, we can celebrate how we are going to end up, rather than fret about what we have to endure. God wants us to prosper and to give us hope and a future. He will work all things together for our good. He will complete whatever He begins. Philippians 1:6 says, "Being confident of this very thing, that He Who has begun a good work in you will complete it until the day of Jesus Christ."

Jesus not only knew of the plan God had for His life, but He also lived with the understanding of the anointing that was on His life. The anointing was the empowerment that enabled Him to live His life on this earth with the authority of His Father. We need the anointing of God. We simply cannot life this life without it. The anointing is the power of God that is given to us by way of the Holy Spirit, in order to do the will of God. It is God's power that is released in us by way of the Holy Spirit, so we may give glory and honor to God. One of the things the devil

Glimpses of Grace

could not handle was the anointing upon Jesus' life. When there are things that are in the plan of God that causes discomfort and stress, God will give the anointing to handle it. There are things that happened in our lives that would have destroyed us if it had not been for the anointing of the Holy Spirit. It is a reality that comes by having Jesus in your life. The Holy Spirit enables you to serve, in spite of your feelings. You worship when you don't feel like it, and you witness when you don't feel like it. It has nothing to do with your feelings.

Pray for the Lord to fill you with the "humility of the Lamb (Jesus)." Pick up your towel and serve as Jesus served. Whatever God has planned for you, walk in the anointing and wash the feet of those whom the Lord will put in your path: it's a part of God's plan. Do it in the love of Jesus, as though you belong to "The Order of The Towel."

SPEAK TO YOUR MOUNTAIN

> "For verily I say unto you, That whosoever shall say unto this mountain, Be thou removed, and be thou cast into the sea; and shall not doubt in his heart, but shall believe that those things which he saith shall come to pass; he shall have whatsoever he saith. Therefore I say unto you, What things soever ye desire, when ye pray, believe that ye receive them, and ye shall have them." (Mark 11:23-24)

We all have some kind of mountain in our life, but did you know that you can speak to whatever kind of mountain it may be, and if you have faith to believe what you say will come to pass, it will happen? That's what Jesus told His disciples, and He never told a lie. After He had cursed the fig tree for not having fruit on it, it withered away, and the disciples were amazed that it happened. Jesus told them they could do the same thing if they had faith to believe what they say. So many times we say we want something, we pray about it, and then we don't really believe it will come to pass. We can't pray and expect God to grant what we ask if we don't believe He will do it. Without faith, it is impossible to please Him.

I remember a story I heard years ago, about a woman who wanted to test God on this mountain-moving faith. So, she had a tree in her yard that she wanted removed. She spoke to the tree and told it to be removed from her yard by the next morning. The next morning, she ran to her window to see if the tree was still there; and it was still there. She remarked, "I knew it!" Now what does that tell you? When she spoke to the tree, she didn't expect it to be removed in the morning. She said that she knew it would still be there. She spoke with no faith to believe! When Jesus spoke to that fig tree, He didn't expect for it to be still alive when He returned.

Alright, what mountains do you need to be removed from your life? A broken marriage to be restored? A job with better benefits? You need a job? You want to see your children saved? Your health restored? Reconciliation in a relationship? What is it you need God to do that is a looming mountain in your life? Our words are life when we speak them with faith, believing and trusting God to work it out. That is unlimited power! Go to the Word of God, find the Scripture that applies to your mountain, speak the Word of God over your mountain and decree and declare that it is removed. Jesus said when you pray, believe that you already have what you are asking. That is faith in action. No mountain is too high, too wide, or too deep that Jesus cannot move it. Speak to your mountain!

Glimpses of Grace

"And this is the confidence that we have in Him, that, if we ask any thing according His will, He heareth us: and if we know that He hear us, whatsoever we ask, we know that we have the petitions that we desired of Him." (I John 5:14-15.)

THE MAJESTIC HANDIWORK OF GOD

The Word of God says that the fool has said in his heart there is no God. He doesn't regard the Almighty God or acknowledge Him in any way. He totally rejects who God is. And do you know why? Because it is so easy to say there is no God and feel they are not accountable to a Holy God. If they say He doesn't exist, then they feel they don't have to obey Him. That is why the Bible calls that kind of a person a fool. How can anyone look at the wonders God has put all around us; the great lofty mountains that loom up towards the sky in all of their glory and their beautiful colors; some red, some black, some white with snow; some covered with beautiful wildflowers. Who can truthfully behold the majesty of God in His handiwork and say there is no God? We are all proof there is a living God.

Just take a good look at these bodies we live in. Everything in beautiful, perfect order, functioning and coordinated together. Imagine what you would look like if your toes were growing out of your head, or one eye was on your hand and the other on your foot? Or what if your leg was where your nose is, or if God had made your mouth in the middle of your back? Yes, it was God our Creator who put us together and we are His handiwork. "I will praise Thee; for I am fearfully and wonderfully made: marvelous are Thy works; and that my soul knoweth right well." (Ps. 139:14). It was no big bang, or something that came out of the ocean and evolved into human beings. One would have to be mindless to believe such foolishness. Every time someone sets out to prove there is no God, they end up proving He does truly exist, and that He always has been, and that He is from everlasting to everlasting.

God is a God of order, and He has great plans for each one of His creations. He created us to do great things for His glory, and no matter what path we take or what choices we make, good or bad, God's plan will stand. We have to submit to the will of God if we want to live the abundant life that Jesus died to give us. He created us in His own image and gave us dominion over everything He created. (See Gen. 1:26). But man relinquished his dominion and gave it to another (Satan). Because of his great love for His creation, God sent His Son, Jesus Christ, to die for the sin of man, thereby setting things back into His order. As we receive the finished work on Calvary, God once again sees us as a part of His majestic handiwork. "Worthy are You, our Lord and God, to receive glory and honor and power, for You created all things, and by Your will they existed and were created." (Rev. 4:11. ESV)

THE LIGHT OF THE WORLD IS JESUS

Jesus came into a world full of darkness, dark with rampant sin and no regard for Almighty God. He came to be a Light in our darkness. "In Him was life; and the life was the light of men. And the Light shineth in darkness; and the darkness comprehended it not." (John 1:4-5). Think of a room with gross darkness, no light shining anywhere. Then, someone comes in and lights a match, a tiny match. That darkness has to give way to the light of that match. If this could happen with a very small match, how much more can the Light of Jesus push back the darkness in our lives. The darkness in that room had to acknowledge the light had come, and so we must acknowledge that Jesus, the Light of the world, has come. He wants to shine in our lives with His love, joy, and peace. In Him is no darkness at all, He is the true Light, which lighteth every man (See John 1:9). Jesus says whoever follows Him will never again walk in darkness, He gives new life; life to the blind, the lame, the deaf, and the sinner who He died for. When we obey Him and His way, He, the Sun of Righteousness, shines in our lives and ultimately lives His life through us.

Glimpses of Grace

If only the world would turn to Jesus and receive the finished work on Calvary, what a change it would be in each of our lives. The Word of God says that Jesus is our Light and our Salvation and that we don't have to fear anyone or anything; He is the strength of our life. There is no one greater than our Lord and Savior Jesus Christ. Isn't it wonderful to know that all we have to do is trust Him and know that His Word is true? He is everything we need in life. Let Jesus light up your life. Will you let Him in to be the everlasting light (See Isa. 60:19), the Light that was sent to lighten the Gentiles? (See Luke 2:32). "For You are the fountain of life, the light by which we see." (Ps. 36:9)

THE RIGHT THIRST

Have you ever been so thirsty you felt if you could just get something to drink you would be alright? So, you drink soda, and you find you are still thirsty. Then you drink some juice, and you are still thirsty. No matter what you drink, it doesn't quench that thirst until you drink a glass of nice cold WATER. Water is what quenches that deep yearning, the thirst of our bodies.

In Luke 19:41-42 and 44, the account of Jesus riding into Jerusalem it is written, "And when He was come near, He beheld the city, and wept over it, Saying, If thou hadst known, even thou, at least in this thy day, the things which belong unto thy peace! But now they are hid from thine eyes. …because thou knewest not the time of thy visitation." Jesus wept because Israel did not receive Him, their Messiah Who had come to save them. Now, looking back at Jesus on the cross, we can see His thirst was not for water, but for the souls of mankind. After all, that is why He came to earth. He came to destroy the works of the devil, the enemy of our souls. In this passage, the Lord Jesus Christ was yearning over Israel's salvation, yet Israel didn't even realize her salvation had come. Her deliverance was at hand and by her rejecting Jesus she rejected her freedom. He was thirsting for Israel's deliverance.

Glimpses of Grace

We are not unlike Israel. Jesus wants to give us His love and we reject Him by accepting the lust of the world; running after people, places, and things, and making Him last in our lives. "And thou shalt love the LORD thy God with all thy heart, and with all thy soul, and with all thy mind, and with all thy strength: this is the first commandment. And the second is like, namely this, Thou shalt love thy neighbor as thyself. There is none other commandment greater than these." (Mark 12:30-31). Jesus prayed that we would love Him as the Father loves Him. "…That the love wherewith Thou has loved Me may be in the, and I in them." (John 17:26b). Jesus yearns to fill us with His love. "If a man loves Me, he will keep My words: and My Father will love him, and We will come unto him, and make Our abode with him." (John 15:23)

Jesus thirsts to give us His joy. He said, "These things have I spoken unto you, that My joy might remain in you, and that your joy might be full." (John 16:11). We accept the *happiness* of the world, which lasts only as long as it makes us feel good. Happiness depends on our circumstances. The joy of the Lord dwells deep down in our soul and goes on and on no matter what our circumstances are. Jesus yearns to give us His peace. We instead try to find peace by compromising with the world. The world cries for peace and there is no peace. Jesus is our peace; He is the Prince of Peace. There can be no compromise. "Peace I leave with you, My peace I give unto you: not as the world giveth, give I unto you…" (John 14:17)

Glimpses of Grace

Jesus thirsts for us to be like Him, serving those who are oppressed or with Christ in their lives. We tend to put aside those who are not like us. If they are not as holy as we think we are, we don't want to have anything to do with them. When Jesus healed the leper, He did something unthinkable to the religious leaders in His day. "When He was come down from the mountain, great multitudes followed Him. And, behold, there came a leper and worshipped Him, saying, Lord, if Thou wilt, Thou canst make me clean. Jesus put forth His hand, and touched Him, saying I will; be thou clean. And immediately his leprosy was cleansed." (Matt. 8:1-3). Notice first of all, Jesus had to "come down from the mountain." We want to stay up on the mountain and not touch those down in the valley. Jesus is thirsting for us to reach out to the downtrodden. But we say, "I send this, and I send that…" and Jesus says, "GO"! "GO when you can, GO where you can. Let them see you, let them feel your loving touch!" (See Matt, 28:19).

We have to commit to changed thinking and behavior in order to be like Jesus, and thirst as He thirsts. "Blessed are they which do hunger and thirst after righteousness; for they shall be filled." (Matt. 5:6). Thirst for righteousness because all our righteousnesses are as filthy rags. "But we are all as an unclean thing, and all our righteousnesses are as filthy rags; and we all do fade as a leaf; and our iniquities, like the wind, have taken us away." (Isa. 64:6). The woman at the well realized she needed to change her thirst after she met Jesus. She no longer wanted to thirst for lust, but for the love of God and Jesus, the Living Water. When we yield to the Lord Jesus Christ, He becomes our Righteousness. "But of Him are ye in Christ Jesus, Who of God is made unto us wisdom, and righteousness, and sanctification, and redemption." (1 Cor. 1:30). The Lord Jesus Christ is available to satisfy our thirst. He invites us to come to Him and drink and live. He is available to quench our thirst, but will we offer Him vinegar for His?

THE WORD MADE FLESH

"In the beginning was the Word, and the Word was with God and the Word was God. The same was in the beginning with God. All things were made by Him; and without Him was not anything made that was made. And the Word was made flesh, and dwelt among us, (and we beheld His glory, the glory as of the only begotten of the Father,) full of grace and truth." (John 1:1-3; 14)

The Word of God says that when God created the world, Jesus was right there with Him. When He said, "Let us make man in Our image," Jesus was right there with Him. (See Gen. 1:26). God has always existed in three Persons; God the Father, God the Son (Jesus), and God the Holy Spirit. As you read and study the Word of God (the Bible) you will see all three Persons of the Trinity working at different times. The Gospel of John says that nothing was made without Jesus. When God created, He SPOKE everything into existence. He said, "Let there be," and it was. As He SPOKE, that was Jesus creating things into existence. "So God created man in His Own image,

Glimpses of Grace

in the image of God created He him; male and female created He them." (Gen. 1:27). (The Word is speaking to someone right here.)

When Jesus entered into the world, He entered as the Word of God. That is why He kept saying, "The words I speak, I'm not speaking on My Own, I speak whatever the Father tells Me to speak." (John 7:16; John 12:49). Jesus is still speaking in these last days, and we must heed what He is saying. In days past, God spoke to man through His prophets, but now He is speaking through His Son, Jesus. We have Jesus' example as He walked this earth and we have the written Word, the Bible. "Hath in these last days spoken unto us by His Son, Whom He hath appointed heir of all things, by Whom also He made the worlds; Who being the brightness of His glory, and the express image of His Person, and upholding all things by the Word of His power, when He had by Himself purged our sins, sat down on the right hand of the Majesty on high;" (Heb. 1:2-3)

Jesus, our Creator, came in the flesh, lived, suffered, bled, and died, then rose again. He is now seated at the right hand of the Father, praying for us. (See Rom. 8:34). There is power in His Words when He speaks them, and power in His Words when we speak them. There is power in our own words when we speak them, so be careful what you let out of your mouth. Speaking Jesus' Words will always bring encouragement and hope. Jesus lives within us, and He speaks through us, so open your mouth and let Him fill it with Himself. You will be surprised what a difference we will make in the lives of others when we do. "For the Word of God is quick, and powerful, and sharper than any two-edged sword, piercing even to the dividing asunder of soul and spirit, and of the joints and marrow, and is a discerner of the thoughts and intents of the heart." (Heb. 4:12). (Jesus the Word, knows everything.)

TO FLY LIKE THE EAGLE

The eagle has the longest life-span among birds. It can live up to 70 years. But to reach this age, the eagle has to make a hard decision. In its 40's, its long and flexible talons (those thick long claws) can no longer grab prey which serves as food. Its long, sharp beak becomes bent. Its old-aged and heavy wings, due to their thick feathers, become stuck to its chest and make it difficult to fly. Then, the eagle is left with two options; it can either die or go through a painful process of change which lasts 150 days. The process requires that the eagle fly to a mountain top and sit on its nest. While there, the eagle knocks its beak against a rock until it plucks it out. After plucking it out, the eagle will wait for a new beak to grow back and use the new beak to pluck out its talons. When its new talons grow back, the eagle starts plucking its old-aged feathers, and after five months the eagle takes its famous flight of rebirth and lives for 30 more years. Was it worth it to that eagle to go through 150 days of pain, in order to live 30 more years? I truly think so!

Why is change needed? Many times in our lives we find that in order to survive we have to go through a change process. We sometimes need to get rid of old habits, old memories, and other past traditions, and it is only when we are freed from these past burdens we can take advantage of the present. We walk around spiritually dead until we are willing to let go of the past and live in the present. We walk around holding onto past hurts and feelings, bitterness and anger, and unforgiveness, with a vengeful heart. We are walking around burdened down, dragging grave clothes, and some things that should have been buried a long time ago. We have to let it go and let God take full control of our lives. Think about it, if that eagle chose not to go through that very painful change process, it would surely die. How much do you want to live? Do you want to live the abundant life that Jesus promised? Then be willing to go through the change process. Go up to your mountain top, the place where you are close to God, and stay there until your change comes.

When it rains, most birds run for shelter. The eagle is the only bird that in order to avoid the rain starts flying above the clouds. God wants us to learn to fly above the clouds, where the sun is always shining. Have you ever gone to the airport in the rain and after you take flight you find yourself above the clouds with the sun shining bright? With God, all things are possible! We can fly above the clouds of life. There is a change coming and we have to be ready and willing to make the change. Accept what God allows because He knows exactly what He is doing. He knows how beautiful we will be when He is finished with us. We are going to be brand new like that eagle; able to fly to higher heights of glory with renewed strength and with the eyesight of an eagle, who can see his prey on the ground while flying 1000 feet in the air, eyes focused on the prize so we can see it from afar and by faith we draw it nigh. So, I encourage you to mount up with your new wings like an eagle, take your flight and soar high towards the Son, Jesus Christ the Son of Righteousness with healing in His wings because "earth has no sorrow that heaven cannot heal." (Thomas Moore). Whatever struggles you are going through, whatever you are holding on to, let it go and let God take you to higher plains than you can ever imagine. It will be worth it all!

> "He giveth power to the faint; and to them that have no might He increaseth strength. But they that wait upon the LORD shall renew their strength; they shall mount up with wings as eagles; they shall run, and not be weary; and they shall walk, and not faint." (Isa. 40:29 & 31)

TOUCHING JESUS WITH A PURPOSE

Jesus was on His way to heal a little girl, Jairus' daughter, when He had an encounter with a woman looking for a miracle. The Word says, "As soon as she came up behind Jesus and barely touched His clothes, her bleeding stopped." Jesus said to the woman, "You are now well because of your faith. Many God give you peace!" (Luke 8:43-44). Most of us may be familiar with the story of the woman who had been suffering with pain and bleeding for 12 years. She had spent all of her money on doctors, and had only gotten worse over the years. I am sure she had heard about Jesus and His healing miracles, and purposed in her heart that if she could just touch the hem of His garment, she knew she would be made well. Wherever Jesus went, there was a crowd around Him, and He had gotten caught up in this crowd while on His way to Jairus' home. The woman was also in that crowd, with the determination to get close enough to Jesus to touch His robe. According to the Jewish Law, she was not even supposed to be in public with an issue of blood, much more was it forbidden that she should *touch* a Rabbi! But she had a purpose! She was pressing toward her miracle! She had to receive her miracle, which meant she believed

Glimpses of Grace

Jesus; she believed everything she knew about Him, and everything she ever heard Him say.

Do we believe everything like that? Do we have that kind of faith to believe what God has said? Faith to believe what we know about Him? What do you know about Jesus? What has He done in your life? What has He said to you? Do you believe it? Or do you believe that it is a waste of time to believe what you do not see? This woman had no doubt in her mind that she was going to be healed when she touched Jesus' garment. She didn't say, *"Maybe I will be healed."* She said, *"If I could just touch the hem of His garment, I **know** I will me made whole again."* Instantly, as soon as she touched Him, she stopped bleeding! She was healed after 12 years of going to doctors, with no results. Jesus said, *"Who touch Me!"* And His disciples said, *"With all this crowd, and You're asking, 'Who touched Me?'"* Jesus said virtue had gone out of Him. This woman had received her miracle. Jesus told her that her faith had made her whole. (See Mark 5:25-34). That's the kind of faith that moves the heart of God. When we fast and pray with a purpose, with the determination to touch Jesus, He says, "Ask what ye will and it shall be done unto you." (See John 15:7). God just wants to know that we know Him, that we know He is able to do what we ask of Him, and that we **trust** Him to do it. This woman had heard of Jesus and the great and mighty works He was doing among the people. That's all she needed to know! Her reasoning was that if He did it for others, I know He'll do it for me. There was no doubt at all; she had great faith and she activated her faith by taking the risk of condemnation by touching Jesus.

Are you willing to take the risk, lay your life on the line, and trust God with all your heart? What is it you want Him to do for you? What miracle do you need Him to perform in your life or for someone you are praying? I'm sure many of us have seen God move in our life and the life of others when we touched Jesus, expecting a miracle. We have petitions on the altar, spoken and unspoken, that we are fasting and praying for, expecting the manifestation of the move of God on our behalf, and expecting to see the miracle of God in our situation. We can't afford to waiver or doubt in our faith. We can't let people and things get in our way. We have to be determined just as that woman with the issue of blood. We have issues in our lives that only Jesus can handle. We know Who Jesus is and we have seen Him work. He is the same yesterday, today, and forever. He never changes. What He has done in the past, He will do today. Though it's tarry, wait for it, it will surely come; be patient (in the waiting room). No matter what it looks like, keep claiming your miracle. What God has for us is for us and nobody can take it away. Reach up and touch the hem of Jesus' garment with a purpose, decreeing and declaring that God is going to work in your situation, for your good and for His glory! Hallelujah!

Keep saying what God has already said. He said that if we "trust Him, we will never miss out on any good thing."

(See Romans 8:28). He is always working for the good of those who love Him because we are the ones He has chosen for His purpose. "Trust the Lord and follow Him. He will give you the desires of your heart." (Ps. 37:4). If we learn to say what God says, and lean not on our own understanding, God will honor our faith and give us what we desire, according to His will. Determine to push through the crowd of doubt, fear, defeat, and worry, and look at the circumstances instead of at Jesus, the Problem Solver. Touch Jesus with a purpose and expect to be healed in every area of your life: spiritually, physically, mentally, and financially. According to your faith be it unto you. Receive your miracle blessing!

WHEN GOD BREATHES IN YOUR DIRECTION

The same wind that seemingly is blowing you in so many negative ways and blowing all kinds of trouble, disappointments, pain, and suffering into your life, is the same breath of God that is blowing you into the predestination He has set up for your life. You are predestined and foreordained for good works. God is building character in you. He is building integrity, strengthening your faith, building trust and patience, and setting you up for a blessing. "A blessing?," you say, "Well it sure doesn't look like it from where I stand." That's because you can't see what the future holds for you. You can't see what lies beyond the bend in the road, but God can.

Joseph didn't know what was in store for him in the future, but God had great plans for his life. He went through tests, trials, and great tribulation while in prison for years, but he never turned his back on God and God did not turn His back on Joseph. He remained true and humble before God, and God gave him the grace he needed for each and every day. "Be He giveth more grace. Wherefore He saith, God resisteth the proud, but giveth grace unto the humble. Submit yourselves therefore to God. Resist the devil, and he will flee from you. Draw nigh to God, and He will draw nigh to you… Humble yourselves in the sight of the Lord, and He shall lift you up." (James 4:6-8a; 10). Joseph had no idea that he was being set up for a great blessing and to be a blessing to many for generations to come. Do you realize there is not one word of Joseph complaining about his plight or blaming God or anyone for where he ended up in Egypt? He patiently endured all he went through, and God was able to use him right where he was. (See Gen. 39-50)

Is God blowing His breath in your direction? If you are feeling a strain in your life, don't complain and don't blame anyone, just know that it is God moving you in position to be blessed, and go humbly and willingly. That strong wind is God's breath, breathing new life into you. Accept what God is allowing to come your way, then thank and praise Him for the glory that is on the way. What you are going through cannot be compared to the glory He has in store for you and for many others in your life. "For I reckon that the sufferings of this present time are not worthy to be compared with the glory which shall be revealed in us. And we know that all things work together for good to them that love God, to them who are the called according to His purpose." (Rom. 8:18; 28)

THE KINGDOM OF GOD, HERE AND NOW

All of us have prayers on the altar we are expecting God to answer. We're seeking Him, calling on Him, petitioning Him day after day, and we find that things seem worse than when we started. Things are breaking down, falling apart, going to pieces, and we wonder why, or what in the world is happening?! God requires something of us. We read it in Matthew 6:33, "But seek ye first the kingdom of God, and His righteousness; and all these things shall be added unto you." Jesus said that if we ask anything in His Name, it shall be done for us by His Father in heaven. He also said, "You do what I want you to do first. You be obedient to My assignment for you, then I will give you what you want. You give Me what I want, first, then I will give you the desires of your heart. When your purpose line up with My purpose for your life, then I will bless you with abundant blessings." (See John 10:10b; John 15:7; 2 Corinthians 9:8). God has equipped us with the tools we need to fulfill His plan and purpose in His Kingdom, and if we do nothing, we are saying to God, "You haven't given me anything to work with." So, we make Him a liar because He said, "But ye shall receive power, after that the Holy Ghost is come upon you: and ye shall be witnesses unto

Glimpses of Grace

Me…" (See Acts 1:8). Jesus said He has given us power over all the powers of the enemy. His Word says, "(For the weapons of our warfare are not carnal, but mighty through God to the pulling down of strong holds;) casting down imaginations, and every high thing that exalteth itself against the knowledge of God, and bringing into captivity every thought to the obedience of Christ; ***and having in a readiness to revenge all disobedience, when your obedience is fulfilled.***" (2 Corinthians 10:4). Do you realize we do not quote the last part of that Scripture because there is no period until we get to the last part. In other words, we need to practice what we preach. When we become doers of the Word that we preach, when we are obedient to the will of God for our lives, then we can expect God to move on our behalf and touch those souls we are praying for. "The Lord gave the Word; great was the company of those that published it." (Ps. 68:11). We are all members of God's publishing company. A publishing company publishes and distributes the word.

The Holy Ghost breathed the Seed of the Word of God into the womb of the virgin Mary. The Word grew inside of her and in the fullness of time, the Word came forth and began to contaminate all who were willing to get close to Him, the Man Jesus Christ, in the flesh. He walked this earth, giving of Himself to everyone who would believe and receive Him. Jesus was full of the Father, He was filled up with God and He said whoever receives Him, receives Him who sent Him. He came to glorify His Father and to bring mankind back to God. He said, "The words that I speak, I speak not of Myself but I speak the words that My Father tell Me to speak." (See John 12:49-50). When we speak, we are not speaking our own words, we are speaking the words the Father has given. When we, like Mary, become impregnated with the Word of God, in the fullness of time that Word has to come forth. In order to become impregnated, we must have a very intimate relationship with Jesus; day and night, reading and studying Him, the Word of God, and spending time talking to Him and listening to Him. The more we spend time with the Word, the bigger He will become in us, until we won't be able to contain Him. We will be like Jeremiah, "It's like fire shut up in my bones. I can't keep it in any longer; I've got to get it out, I've got to share it, show it, publish it, distribute it: tell it everywhere I go!!!" (See Jer. 20:9). And many who are walking in darkness will see the light of the Word in our lives and want to embrace it.

Every mother who brings forth a baby into this world is already equipped to nourish that baby with breast milk, so it can feed and grow. She has been equipped to nurture and love that baby with the love of God He has put in her heart. God has given her the wisdom she needs to train up that child to follow the ways of the Kingdom. However, if she lets her milk dry up (and it will dry up if you don't use it), and if she doesn't keep eating the right foods, feeding on the Word of God, herself, that mother will have nothing to give out. Her body will become depleted and incapable of nourishing anyone. We are the Body of Christ, the Church, and God has equipped us with the tools we need to feed the world His Kingdom. His Kingdom is righteousness and peace and joy in the Holy Ghost! (See Rom. 14:17). We have Jesus our Savior on the inside, we have the Holy Ghost to empower us, guide us, direct us, and bring us back to remembrance of the things Jesus has spoken to us, so we can give it out to others. If we don't use what we have, it will dry up inside of us and we will not have done what Jesus has commissioned us to do; to go into all the world and preach the Gospel to all nations, teaching them to observe all things He has commanded us. (See Matt. 28:18-20). The Church needs to get back to doing the first works, which is to proclaim the Gospel of Jesus Christ so that souls will be brought into the Kingdom of God. Win the lost at any cost, and there is a cost! We must be willing to take up our cross daily and follow Jesus. Crucify and get rid of self and die daily so that others might live. We are to teach that Jesus Christ came into this world as a male child, lived, suffered, died for the sin of all mankind, was buried, and rose again. That is the Gospel in a nutshell. Because of this, everyone, regardless of race, color, or creed now has the opportunity to become a part of the Kingdom of God, right here on earth and eternally in heaven.

The Kingdom of God is Jesus. He is our righteousness, He is our peace, and He is our joy. We love Him because He first loved us! He came to give us abundant

Glimpses of Grace

life right here on earth. He came to bring the order of His Father on earth as it is in heaven. We pray it all the time, "Thy Kingdom come. Thy will be done on earth as it is in heaven." That is the main Kingdom Principal; that is the order of God. Just as the angels in heaven are obeying the will of the Father, so shall it be here on earth. Those of us who in this life follow the will of God, will enjoy all the promises He has made to those who obey His will, and to those who love and follow Him. That's the Kingdom of God, here and now.

WHAT KIND OF CHRISTIAN ARE YOU?

What do people see when they see us? Do they know we are Christians? Many times we don't have to say anything in order for people to recognize the Christ in us. In Jesus' day, the Pharisees wore certain clothing that made them stand out in the crowd. They walked a certain way and talked a certain way with their strict observances of the written law. They considered themselves high above the "common" people. Everyone who saw them knew they were Pharisees. On the other hand, the apostles looked no different than all the other people. On the outside they looked like everyone else, but it was who was on the inside that made the difference as they walked and talked among the people. They spoke with boldness and performed miracles in the presence of the people. When the religious leaders heard the apostles and saw the miracle of the man who was healed, they were amazed those men hadn't been to school, they didn't have any degrees, and just listened to them; look at the miracle they performed. Oh yes, those men had been with Jesus, no doubt about it. Remember, this was after the Holy Ghost came and filled them. Their boldness was the Holy Ghost dwelling on the inside of them, their words were the Holy Ghost speaking through them. As followers of Jesus Christ, our lives should be showing the same manifestation of the Holy Ghost. The world should be able to see Jesus in us and be drawn to Him. We represent the Lord Jesus Christ, and everything we say and do should look like we belong to Him.

How do we treat other Christians? In the church there are those who consider themselves above those who have no titles, just as the Pharisees did. They judge new Christians instead of encouraging them. They criticize the way they dress, the way they talk, even knowing the new Christian needs to be taught and discipled in order to learn the ways of the Kingdom of God. We can chase the new Christians away by the way we treat them with lack of love and compassion. The church is the "hospital" for the sick, the hopeless, the downtrodden, the hurting, the brokenhearted, and those who have no helper. How do we treat them? Where is the love of God? Do we greet them with a smile, a hug, or a word of cheer and encouragement? Would they be able to say they were blessed by being in our presence? Some of us tend to look at people through the eyes of flesh instead of through the eyes of Jesus. We look at their outward appearance and make quick judgements. We need to realize that every person on this earth is a soul that Jesus died for, and when we come in contact with anyone, that is how we should treat them. Jesus didn't pick and choose who He was going to love, who He was going to forgive, or who He was going to heal. Are we better than He? If the world can't see Jesus in us, where are they going to see Him? The apostles were noted to have "turned the world upside down." We too, should be turning this world upside down by reflecting the love of Jesus everywhere we go. What kind of Christian are you? "Now when they saw the boldness of Peter and John, and perceived that they were unlearned and ignorant men, they marveled; and they took knowledge of them, that they had been with Jesus." (Acts 4:13)

WHO LOVES YA', BABY?

"In this was manifested the love of God towards us, because that God sent His only begotten Son into the world, that we might live through Him." (1 John 4:9).

Do you remember the old television police series "Kojak," with Telly Savalas as the bald, lollipop sucking, tough guy detective? Always, in each drama he would end up saying, "Who loves ya', Baby?" If you were asked that question today, what would be your answer? I think I would start singing the song I learned in my early childhood and taught my children, *"Jesus loves me this I know, for the Bible tells me so. Little ones to Him belong, they are weak, but He is strong. Yes, Jesus loves me; yes, Jesus loves me; yes, Jesus loves me: for the Bible tells me so."* (Anna Bartlett Warner)

God our Father has made it so clear in His Word that He loves us unconditionally. We are His children, and He will always desire the best for us; it is His desire to give us the Kingdom. Every day He has new mercies waiting for us to demonstrate His love through us. God has said, "Call unto Me, and I will answer thee, and shew thee great ad mighty things, which thou knowest not." (Jer. 33:3). Oh, yes, He loves you and me, He gave His life for us. He was willing to take off His robe of glory and put on the garment of human flesh to live, suffer, and die a death we should have died because of our sin. "Greater love hath no man than this, that a man lay down his life for his friends." (John 15:13). How many friends do you have that will be willing to lay down their lives for you? True love demonstrates itself in action. You know the old adage, *"Action speaks louder than words."* There is great truth in that. Jesus is love, personified; if we want to know what love looks like, just look at Jesus. In all His ways and actions, He gave us the example of love. If you ever feel unloved, just reach out to Jesus. He is always waiting with outstretched arms to receive you. He doesn't love us because we are loving and kind, always looking good, smelling good, or sounding good. Jesus said there is none good but one, and that is God. He loves the unlovable, the angry, downtrodden, the stinking, the dirty, and the one that no one else would dare to love. There is nothing we can say or do to make the Father love us, and nothing we can say or do that will make Him stop loving us. He loves us because that is who He is. He is God and God is love. "He that loveth not knoweth not God, for God is love." (I John 4:8.) And now you know. "Nay, in all these things we are more than conquerors through Him that loved us. For I am persuaded, that neither death, not life, no angels, nor principalities, nor powers, nor things present, nor things to come, Nor height, nor depth, nor any other creature, shall be able to separate us from the love of God, which is in Christ Jesus our Lord." (Rom. 8:37-39)

REJOICE IN THE LORD

> "This day is holy unto the LORD your God; mourn not, nor weep. For all the people wept, when they heard the words of the law. Then he said unto them, Go your way, eat the fat, and drink the sweet, and send portions unto them for whom nothing is prepared: for this day is holy unto our Lord: neither be ye sorry; for the joy of the LORD is your strength." (Neh. 8:9b-10)

This event takes place after Nehemiah goes back to Jerusalem from Babylon, where he had been taken captive by King Nebuchadnezzar. After Nehemiah had rebuilt the wall, the people asked Ezra, the scribe, to read the Book of the Law which God given to Moses. After Ezra read all day to the people, they began to cry and be sorrowful because they were able to understand the Word of God like never before. Ezra encouraged them not to be sad, but to rejoice and celebrate because they were now back in Jerusalem and could go to their own cities to live. He told them that, "The joy of the LORD is their strength." (See Neh. 8:10).

This is true when we hear the Word of God and understand what God is saying. It activates the joy of

Glimpses of Grace

the Lord within us, and we gain more strength for the journey. Nehemiah's enemies tried to intimidate him by lying on him and trying to make him afraid while he was rebuilding the wall. Whenever change and progress are underway, there is always going to be competition arising to challenge the leader. The leader has the option to choose whether to turn and run or stand up to the challenge. Nehemiah chose to stand up to the adversary by calling on God and asking for His help. Nehemiah then turned his enemies over to God and asked God to deal with them. (We can choose our battle, to fight or not to fight.) So, he went on to complete the task the Lord gave him to do. Completing that wall gave notice to all adversaries that the Israelites were back. The wall was completed in fifty-two days in spite of opposition, and the adversaries had to acknowledge that only God could have done that. "This is the LORD's doing; it is marvelous in our eyes." (Ps. 118:23). The joy of the LORD was Nehemiah's strength; the joy of knowing that God was for him and who could be against him; the joy of knowing his mission was accomplished, the wall was rebuilt, and the enemy could no longer come in and ravage the city of Jerusalem.

Sometimes, we as Christians are knocked down and saddened by our adversities of this life, but Jesus encourages us to, "Be of good cheer (rejoice and be glad; be filled with My joy) because I have overcome the world." (John 16:33). When the disciples were saddened because Jesus told them He was going away, He said to them that when

He comes back their joy would be as a mother who had been in pain before childbirth, and when the child is born the mother is filled with joy and forgets all about the pain. (See John 16:20-22.) In this life, we experience all kinds of pain and sorrow; in our homes, with our family, on the job, in our communities, and even in our churches. When we call on Jesus, and by faith stand on His Word and watch Him come and move in every situation, His joy floods our soul, we forget about the pain and suffering, and we come back with more strength than we had before. Fortified! Watch out, devil! "May the God of hope fill you with joy and peace as you trust in Him, so that you may overflow with hope by the power of the Holy Spirit." (Rom. 15:13)

STICKS AND STONES

Remember the old saying, "Sticks and stones may break my bones but words will never hurt me?" Well, the Bible tells us that words have great power and the things we say can mean either life or death. The Epistle of James tells us that we can say very hurtful things out of our mouths that can cause great damage in the lives of others and in our own lives. "But the tongue no man can tame; it is an unruly evil, full of deadly poison. Therewith bless we God, even the Father; and therewith curse we men, which are made after the similitude of God. Out of the same mouth proceedeth blessing and cursing. My brethren, these things ought not so to be." (James 3:8-10). How many times have you said something to someone to hurt them, then wish you hadn't said it? We can't take back words we speak out of our mouths, but we can allow the Holy Spirit to have control over our tongue. We need to practice being slow to speak, and don't blurt out the first thing that comes in your mind. Will it be pleasing to God? How will it affect those around me? Do I really need to say what I am about to say? How many of us stop and think before we speak? I Peter 3:10 says, "For he that will love life, and see good days, let him refrain his tongue from evil, and his lips that they speak no guile."

The thoughts we think in our minds become the words we speak out of our mouths. When we have our minds filled up with Word of God, that will be uppermost in the words that come out of our mouths. Our words are alive, and they can change things, people, situations, circumstances, and the atmosphere around us. If you want a good change, think good thoughts and then words that build up and edify will come out of your mouth. "Do not let any unwholesome talk come out of your mouths, but only what is helpful for building others up according to their needs, that it may benefit those who listen." (Eph. 4:29 NIV)

We must be so very careful about the words we speak into the lives of our children. No matter how they act, speak words of encouragement, and words that will make them feel good about themselves. So many children hear nothing but cursing and words that tear them down, telling them they are no good and will amount to nothing. Why are we surprised when they end up living that kind of life? "The soothing tongue is a tree of life, but a perverse tongue crushes the spirit." (Prov. 15:4 NIV). Change the way you speak, and let your thoughts and conversation be filled with the Word of God. There is nothing more life-changing than the Word of God. It is power packed with faith, love, and hope. When we speak these words into our own life and the lives of others, watch conditions change circumstances, situations, and people. "Let your conversation be always full of grace, seasoned with salt, so that you may know how to answer everyone." (Col. 4:6 NIV)

YOUR MIRACLE IS ON ITS WAY

Our God is a God of miracles. All of creation is a miracle of God. In the beginning, God spoke, and He said, "Let there be," and the light came into being, the sun, moon, and stars. He said, "Let there be," and all living creatures filled the earth. That was a miracle. Look at your hands, your fingers, and how they manipulate and grasp hold of things. Think about all the parts of your body and how everything was made to function, working together to give you the miracle of life. Think about that tiny seed, invisible to the naked eye, that we all came from. How that tiny seed begins to grow in the mother's womb and great God Almighty knows every part before it is formed in the womb. Then it takes nine months forming and growing in the mother's womb before it comes forth at the appointed time (the doctor gives a "due date"). This miracle of God, waiting to come forth. God is the only One who can perform miracles. He is the God of the impossible. There is absolutely nothing He cannot do, but fail – God cannot fail.

I believe we all have a prayer on the altar that seems impossible for a breakthrough, something we can't see how that prayer can be answered. We know it will take

Glimpses of Grace

nothing short of a miracle for that prayer to be answered. How many of you know God is still in the miracle working business? He hasn't changed, He is the same yesterday, today, and forever. All you have to do is believe, believe God, believe He is who He says He is, and believe He will do what He says He will do. Trust Him and His Word. Those prayers you have on the altar, trust God that this is your season for your miracle, and it's time for your baby to come forth. This is the appointed time for you to reap what you have sown; that seed you sowed in tears. It's now time for you to reap with joy. Your miracle is on the way and this is no time to give up and stop believing. When the battle gets tougher, just know that it means your miracle is just that much closer. Your location is not your destiny. It doesn't matter where you are now, and it doesn't matter what it looks like. All hell may be breaking loose, but just know, without a shadow of a doubt, there will be glory after this! When it looks like things are getting worse, the more you pray, pray even harder, pray more, it just means your miracle is about to happen. Just as that pregnant mother to-be begins to have unbearable pain as the baby moves down the birth canal, and she is screaming in agony but still pushing because she knows the harder she pushes she is helping her miracle to come forth.

Keep pushing saints no matter how much it may hurt, keep pushing because your miracle is on its way, and it is about to be made manifest in your life. Every man and tempting devil will have to acknowledge that only

Glimpses of Grace

God could have done it. Loved ones saved, that one who you thought would never say, "yes," to Jesus, relationships restored according to the will of God, and debts paid, and you don't know how it was done accept that it was a miracle of God. Doors opening that no man can shut, favor on every side, prison doors opening, an abundant amount of money coming into your hands. Miracles bursting out all around us. They are coming, "wait for it, it shall surely come." Just hold on a little while longer. Keep praying, keep fasting, keep praising, keep trusting, and keep expecting. "For the Lord had made the host of the Syrians to hear a nose of chariots, and a noise of horses, even the noise of a great host: and they said one to another, Lo, the king of Israel hath hired against us the kings of the Hittites, and the kings of the Egyptians, to come upon us. Wherefore they arose and fled in the twilight, and left their tents and their horses, and their asses, even the camp as it was, and fled for their life." (2 Kings 7:6-7). Your miracle is on its way!

GIVE IT ALL TO JESUS

"And ye shall seek Me, and find Me, when ye shall search for Me with all your heart." (Jer. 29:13)

Many people are proud of themselves to be able to give great speeches and sound important. God is not impressed by our eloquent speech and big words or being able to draw a crowd. Those things do not move Him. Paul said, "I came not with excellency of speech or of wisdom, declaring unto you the testimony of God." (I Cor. 2:1). God is moved by the heart that feels the burdens of this world and brings them to the altar. When we see the news and can pray and intercede for those in need, that is what moves Him. A selfless heart, a heart that is turned toward Him, a heart that seeks Him completely. He wants us to give our whole heart to Him, trusting Him without a shadow of doubt. God wants us to turn everything totally over to Him. He said according to your faith be it unto you. God wants to bless us more than we can imagine. He said we shall receive, if we ask trusting and believing that He will do what we ask. Seeking Him with the whole heart, nothing wavering, that is what moves the heart of God. We have to be expectant, knowing that He will. Our confidence in prayer is not based on our ability to speak, it is based on His ability to hear and understand what we are asking. He has great plans for us and we must expect Him to do great things for us. We limit God, forgetting there is nothing He cannot do. God is the solution to our every problem; He has no problems. We can cast our burdens on Him and know that He knows just what to do with them. He has our back, and He will not leave us alone. He wants us to give our total lives to Him; our children, our finances, our marriage, our jobs, every sickness, or whatever we are carrying as a heavy burden. We cannot carry these loads. Jesus said, "Take My yoke upon you, and learn of Me; for My yoke is easy and My burden is light." (See Matt. 11:29-30). Why should we even want to try to work it out on our own, knowing that we have a God Who never fails? He is our Mighty Fortress, a Way Maker, our Healer, our Peace; let Him be who He is in your life. Acknowledge Him in all your ways and let Him direct your path. Follow His lead, He gives us each day to give it back to Him. He is more than able to undertake and intervene on our behalf. God is a very present help in time of trouble. He is right here with us and will be with us every step of the way if we trust Him. He wants to give us His peace in every situation. Think about who He says He is: He is our Shepherd, the Bread of Life, the Fount of Living Water, The Bright and Morning Star, our Light in the darkness, the Lifter up of our head, the Way the Truth and the Life, and more. Who wouldn't want to serve and trust a God like that? Who is

Glimpses of Grace

He in your life? Is He everything you need? Most of all, is He first in your life? When we put Him first we will have no problem giving it all to Jesus, everything in our lives; knowing that God can, and God will.

LIFE-CHANGING PRAYERS

When we pray in the power of the Holy Ghost, which is that dynamite explosive power, everything is affected around us. First of all, it blows away things on the inside of us and then it explodes out of us and touches everything around us. The Holy Ghost is the One who enables us to pray in the will of the Father. When we pray in the Spirit, we are praying above that which we understand because we are praying with the mind of Christ, who is equal with the Father, because Jesus and the Father are one. The Father says that His ways are not our ways neither are His thoughts our thoughts, for as the heaven is higher than the earth so are His ways higher than our ways and His thoughts higher than our thoughts. Don't try to figure God out, just pray whatever the Holy Spirit leads you to pray. When Jesus' disciples came to Him and asked Him to teach them how to pray, Jesus told them to say, "Our Father, Which art in heaven, Hallowed be Thy Name." This is the model prayer that Jesus taught His disciples to say when they pray. The Lord's Prayer is John 17, the prayer Jesus prayed just before He went to the Garden of Gethsemane.

This prayer that Jesus taught His disciples to pray is power packed! In spreading the Gospel of Jesus Christ, the disciples preached and prayed, and the Scripture says in Acts 17:6, "These have turned the world upside down." Paul and Silas were preaching up a storm in Thessalonica and I'm sure they were also praying up a storm, and Paul, having been taught by Jesus while in the desert, I'm sure was also taught how to pray even as Jesus taught the disciples. Now, if their prayers were turning the world upside down, shouldn't we, too, be turning the world upside down with our prayers? I remember my former pastor, who lived to be 103 years old, asked me one day if I was turning my world upside down with this prayer. She taught me how we can take any person, place, or thing we are praying for, and put them in the middle of this prayer, and know without a shadow of a doubt God is going to answer because we are praying the way He taught us to pray. We can pray, "Thy kingdom come, Thy will be done in my husband; my brother; my sister; my children; because in Your kingdom, Father, there is salvation, healing, peace, deliverance…" Pray whatever you need God's kingdom to come in, and His will to be done in. But in order for this prayer to be effective as we intercede, it must first be effective in our own life. It's not just something we learned by heart as children and now we run through it not even realizing what we are praying. Take time to stop at each phrase and meditate on what you are praying, allow the Holy Spirit to speak to you as you pray these words, and you will feel the power of God permeating in every word. Then, your effective prayers

Glimpses of Grace

will turn your world upside down. "Father, I thank You that You have heard me. I know that You always hear Me." (John 11:42)

KNOW GOD'S POWER THROUGH PRAYER

I think we underestimate the power of prayer. Jesus did a lot of praying as He walked this earth and His disciples realized the power He walked in because they often saw and heard Him pray. That is why they asked Him to teach them how to pray. When they could not cast out the devil from the young man, Jesus told them some things only come out by prayer and fasting. They didn't forget what Jesus taught them, and as we read in the Book of Acts (the Acts of the Holy Ghost through the disciples), they were turning their world upside down. When Jesus gave them His guideline for prayer (See Matt. 6:9-15), they took it and ran with it; they lived it, they believed it, and they shared it. How are we doing?

We cannot pray, "*Our,*" if our faith has no room for others and their needs. We cannot pray, "*Father,*" if we do not demonstrate this relationship to God in our daily living. We cannot pray, "*Who Art in Heaven,*" if all of our interests and pursuits are in earthy things and we are not seeking "those things above." We cannot pray, "*Hallowed be Thy Name,*" if I we are not striving for God's help to be holy. If we are not walking in the holiness of God, acknowledging that He is Holy, we cannot pray for His holiness to be in any situation. We cannot pray, "*Thy Kingdom Come*," if we are not willing to accept God's rule for our life. We cannot pray, "*Thy Will be Done*," if we are unwilling or resentful of having it in our life or if we want to lean unto our own understanding and walk in our own way. After Satan was cast out of heaven, there is no one up there wanting to do their own thing. Nothing but God's will is being done! We cannot pray, "*In Earth as it is in Heaven*," unless we are truly ready to give ourselves to God's service here and now, and we are willing to allow Him to do what He wants to do in these "earthen vessels." We cannot pray, "*Give us This Day Our Daily Bread*," if we are not eating the Bread as Jesus commanded, but are rejecting Jesus, who is the Bread of Life, or if we are withholding from our neighbor the Bread we receive. We cannot pray, "***Forgive Us Our Trespasses as We Forgive Those Who Trespass Against Us***", if we continue to harbor a grudge against anyone and refuse to forgive them. Jesus said His Father will not forgive us if we don't forgive others. We cannot pray, "***Lead Us Not Into Temptation***," if we deliberately choose to remain or put ourselves in a situation where we are likely to be tempted. We can't go knocking on the devil's door and ask God to lead us not into temptation. We cannot pray, "***But Deliver Us From Evil (or The Evil One***)," if we are not prepared to fight the battle having on the Whole Armor of God. We must keep it on at all times, from head to toe (See Eph. 6:10-18). We cannot pray, "***For Thine is the Kingdom***," if we are unwilling to obey the

King. We cannot pray, "***And the Power and the Glory***," it we are seeking power for ourselves and our own glory. We cannot pray, "***Forever***," if we are too anxious about each day's affairs and refuse to lay our burdens down, trusting that all power is in God's hands and there is nothing He cannot do. We cannot pray, "***Amen***," unless we honestly say, "Not my will, but Thy will be done, so let it be."

IN JESUS ALONE

Jesus said, "I am the vine, ye are the branches: He that abideth in Me, and I in him, the same bringeth forth much fruit: for without Me ye can do nothing." (John 15:5). In order to bring in "much" fruit there is a stipulation Jesus put forth. First, we must abide in Him. Abide, what does that mean? We must live in Him and stay where we live. We can't be roaming around out of our dwelling place and expect Jesus to go looking for us. He is only going to look one place, and that is in Him. We must be in close relationship with Him doing His will. He must be living His life through us, otherwise we are no good to Him. "If a man abide not in Me, he is cast forth as a branch, and is withered; and men gather them, and cast them into the fire, and they are burned." (John 15:6)

When we are not abiding in Jesus we are going off on our own way, and there are many ditches on that path. "Trust in the LORD with all thine heart; and lean not on your own understanding. In all thy ways acknowledge Him, and He shall direct thy paths." (Prov. 3:5-6). Jesus said there is nothing we can do without Him. It doesn't matter how smart we think we are, how much education we have, or how much we have prospered without Jesus, it amounts to a big fat "0" in His sight. But whatever we do in His Name, He blesses it abundantly and prospers us in every way. He uses us for His glory and souls are saved, bodies healed, minds delivered from the bondage of addictions, and so much more.

Doing good works out of the will of God will not bring His good favor upon us. Jesus says, "Many will say to Me in that day, Lord, Lord, have we not prophesied in Thy Name? and in Thy Name have cast out devils? And in Thy Name done many wonderful works? And then will I profess unto them, I never knew you: depart from Me, ye that work iniquity." (Matt. 7:22-230. We cannot do God's work without abiding in Jesus; it is unacceptable. Jesus says we must obey His Word and keep His commandments. We can do more if we live in Him and allow Him to live in us. We can do so much more than we ever dreamed we could do. Jesus said that we would do greater works than He did. With the empowerment of the Holy Ghost it is possible, but we cannot bypass Jesus and expect to do the greater works. The Holy Ghost is the One who enables us to live in Jesus, and He is Jesus living in us. He takes the things of Jesus and shows them to us. We cannot bombard our way to the Father and ignore Jesus. He is the only way to the Father, and He will be our Judge in the end. But with Jesus, we can do all things. "I can do all things through Christ Who strengthens me." (Phil. 4:13)

THE FATHER'S HANDWRITING

The great Evangelist, Billy Graham, preached one message for years, all over the world, and because he preached the same simple message, thousands of souls have come to Christ and have been saved. He preached John 3:16, "For God so loved the world, that He gave His only begotten Son, that whosoever believeth in Him should not perish, but have everlasting life." He preached the love and forgiveness of our Father, and this message written to us by the Father will never change. He loves us unconditionally, and in order to receive His forgiveness, we have to acknowledge that we need it. In our Father's message, it says, "If we confess our sins, He is faithful and just to forgive us our sins, and to cleanse us from all unrighteousness." (I John 1:9).

Do you recognize your Father's handwriting? Have you seen His handwriting before? This is what He wrote, "The LORD hath appeared of old unto me, saying, Yea, I have loved thee with an everlasting love: therefore with lovingkindness have I drawn thee." (Jer. 31:3). In spite of the fact that we all have sinned, He still loves us, and we still sin, every day; by thought, word, look, deed, or feeling. We are not perfect, therefore we never live a day without sinning against our Father. We may not even realize we have sinned, but He remembers that we are "dust," and He "pities us" because we are His children. He will never cast us aside or disown us, but He forgives, over and over and over again. Our Father proved how much He loves us and forgives us by sending His only begotten Son, Jesus, to die on Calvary. That is why Jesus cried out from the cross, "Father, forgive them; for they know not what they do." Is there anyone in your life that you just truly haven't forgiven? We say forgiveness is a process, but it really isn't. The process is the purifying of our own heart to act in obedience to the will of the Father. Jesus never taught that forgiveness is a process. It's an act of our will to be willing to forgive.

Have you read the note? Do you recognize your Father's handwriting? It is a simple message, "All is forgiven. Love, Dad" The message has been written to all of us over 2000 years ago, and all we have to do is receive it from our Father. This is the greatest blessing we could ever receive, a message of forgiveness. This is the greatest gift we could ever receive, and this gift is through our Lord and Savior Jesus Christ. Receive it today! "I write unto you little children, because your sins are forgiven you for His Name's sake." (I John 2:12)

NO WEAPON

"The LORD is my light and my salvation; whom shall I fear? The LORD is the strength of my life; of whom shall I be afraid?" (Ps. 27:1)

When God has a mission for us and wants to move us to another level, He moves us out of our comfort zone, and we may find that we have to fight some tough battles. Our enemy doesn't care how he takes us out as long as he thinks he's going to win. But in the midst of the battle, God sends us help. No enemy we face is too big for God to handle.

How many of you know that God always has a plan? He knows just how He is going to help us win the battle, all He asks is that we trust Him and let Him do it His way. We can't pick and choose who we want to teach and train us. God is the One who does the choosing, it's His plan and He knows just how to work it out. There are things God has us go through and we may feel it is senseless and meaningless. *"Why do I have to follow all these rules? It doesn't take all of this to be what I want to be. This teacher doesn't know as much as I know."* All the time, we are talking about the Holy Ghost, whom God has sent to help us. We have to learn how to come down and be humble under the leadership of our Teacher; we have to get it on the inside before it can be manifested on the outside. The Holy Ghost has to teach us the Beatitudes (beautiful attitudes) recorded in Matthew 5th chapter, before they can be manifested in our lives as the "Fruit of the Spirit" in Galatians 5th chapter, and all the time God is working things out for our good! He is moving us up to another level.

We don't have to fear no matter how hard the test may seem. Whether it is sickness, lack of finances, broken relationships, or wayward children, the same Holy Ghost is with us to help us. When we are most weak, God shows Himself strong on our behalf. All He wants is for us to trust Him. The Holy Spirt will teach us techniques that the enemy can't handle. "We are more than conquerors, through Him that loved us." (Rom. 8:37). "Through God we shall do valiantly, for He it is that shall tread down our enemies." (Ps. 108:13). Against all odds, He will make us to come out victoriously! God fully equips us for the battles we have to face. He lets us fight them or He fights them for us; either way, we win!

WAITING ON GOD

"Even though the fig trees have no blossoms, and there are no grapes on the vine; even though the olive crop fails, and the fields lie empty and barren, even though the flocks die in the fields, and the cattle barns are empty. Yet I will rejoice in the LORD! I will be joyful in the God of my salvation. The Sovereign LORD is my strength! He will make me as surefooted as a deer and bring me safely over the mountain." (Hab. 3;17-19)

In this passage of Scripture, we see Habakkuk singing a prayer to God. He's telling God that he has heard about Him and how wonderful and mighty He is. Habakkuk rehearses through all the great and mighty acts God did for the children of Israel in the wilderness. Even though they went through all kinds of plagues, pestilences, and wars, God brought them out. Then, He sings the prayer that no matter what it looks like, He knows he can trust God to bring him safely through every trial and tribulation, and that all he has to do is wait on God. Besides trusting God and turning everything over to Him, waiting on God is one of the most important principles of life and being a Christian. He promises us great blessings, if we just wait on Him. Waiting means remaining in my present position until I hear from God for directions. It doesn't mean sitting around doing nothing, but it means knowing that God knows what He is doing, and allowing Him to do what He needs to do in order for His will to be done in my life.

God is working behind the scenes. You can't see what He is doing, but you have to trust Him. If you don't trust Him you will not wait. You are saying, *"I don't trust His timing, I don't trust His purpose, I don't trust that He knows that He is doing."* Then we step out of our waiting position and run ahead of God, messing up everything. We must learn to wait. Isaiah says, "But they that wait upon the LORD shall renew their strength; they shall mount up with wings as eagles; they shall run, and not be weary; and they shall walk, and not faint." (Isa. 40:31). Waiting renews your strength. It builds up your spiritual muscles so you can endure the trials of life. Not only that, you find that you are strong enough to carry someone else who may be in need of your help. So, you see, when we wait on the Lord, we are not just waiting for ourselves, but God has a plan in it all. Waiting is a process. We must ask God to teach us to wait, and to be willing to wait on Him. Job said, "All the days of my appointed time will I wait, till my change come." (Job 14:14). When we choose not to wait, we miss our blessing.

Glimpses of Grace

God is faithful and will surely keep His promises. Lamentations 3:26 says, "It is good that a man should both hope and quietly wait for the salvation of the LORD.." To quietly wait, means that we are not worrying and fretting about what is taking so long. We wait, believing that it will come to pass. "Though the vision tarry, wait for it." (Hab. 2:3). At the appointed time, we will receive the blessing of the Lord. God has His own time schedule and we can't hurry Him. Wait for His salvation in the midst of your circumstance. He saved the Hebrew men in the fiery furnace; Daniel in the lions' den; David when fighting the lion, the bear, and Goliath; Jesus' disciples in the midst of the storm; and the widow and her son in the famine. God saves us in the midst of every situation and every tribulation, and He brings us out victoriously. Waiting teaches us patience. All the time we are waiting, God is working on us, getting us ready to receive the blessing. Psalm 62:5 says, "My soul, wait thou only upon God; my expectation is from Him." Wait on God and expect Him to do what He says. Believe His Word and know that it is true. If He said it, He will do it; wait on Him.

THE SEASONS OF LIFE

"To every thing there is a season, and a time to every purpose under the heaven." (Eccles. 3:1)

We know that every year there are four seasons; winter, spring, summer, and fall. They are always in that order, never changing. There is a certain time of the year that each of these seasons start, and each season knows when it is their time.

And so, it is with us. We all have our season and a time for everything in our life. Nothing is haphazard about our life. God has it all planned out and He is in complete control. There is nothing that happens in our life without the knowledge of the Father, because it is known to Him before the foundation of the world. The plan for our life has been foreordained and predestined by Almighty God.

God has a purpose. Sometimes He reveals it to us and sometimes He doesn't. We just have to trust Him and know that He knows what He is doing.

One year, it snowed in early spring and not one daffodil or tulip asked God, "What are You doing letting it snow on me?" They just kept on growing, not even being discouraged. Not one little robin decided to fly south again because it snowed. They knew it was their time to be where they were. Timing is so important for each season. The snow cannot fall until it reaches its season. The trees cannot bud until they reach their season. The leaves cannot fall until they reach their season. Mary could not have Baby Jesus until "the fullness of time." Jesus could not die until His time had come. He could not die until He had reached the Cross.

God says, "For I know the plans I have for you.. to give you a future and a hope". (See Jer. 29:11). He says, "My thoughts are not your thoughts, neither are your ways My ways".(See Isa. 55:8).

Wait on the Lord and He will give you the desires of your heart, in your season, in your time. We cannot hurry God, but He is always right on time. When trials and tribulations come in our season, we must keep on growing until we come into full bloom; becoming a beautiful flower in the garden of God, fit for the Master's use. "I know that, whatsoever God doeth, it shall be for ever: nothing can be put to it, nor any thing taken from it: and God doeth it, that men should fear before Him," (Eccles. 3:14)

ABOUT THE AUTHOR

Barbara J. Scott is a mother, grandmother, great grandmother, and great great-grandmother. She has been active in the church for many years in many capacities. She loves the Lord Jesus Christ and desires to please Him by doing His will. This has prompted her to come out of her comfort zone and work on having these writings published so that others may be blessed, encouraged, strengthened, and even come to know and experience the love and grace of God through His Son Jesus Christ.

Milton Keynes UK
Ingram Content Group UK Ltd.
UKHW021403011224
451693UK00012B/894